ADEWALE MAKANJUOLA

MINI IMPORTATION SIMPLIFIED

SECRETS OF MAKING 300% TO 500% IN IMPORTING QUALITY AND CHEAP PRODUCTS

MINI

IMPORTATION SIMPLIFIED

Adewale Makanjuola

assume any responsibility or liability whatsoever for what you choose to do with this information. Use your own judgement.

Any perceived slight of specific people or organizations, and any resemblance to characters living, dead or otherwise, real or fictitious is purely intentional. You are encouraged to print this book for easy reading. However, you use this information at your own risk.

Table of Contents

INTRODUCTION

According to Thomas Edison, "Opportunity is missed by most people because it is dressed in overalls, and looks like work." I have to submit to you that there is nothing worse than missing an opportunity that could have changed your life. I also make bold to say that opportunity abounds everywhere on earth. It does not matter what nation of the world you live in; whether you reside amidst the elite of the developed countries or your abode is with the basest of people in the developing nations; there exists an opportunity for you to change your status quo to what you have always wished it to be. As Thomas Edison has quipped, most people miss this opportunity because it is disguised as work.

It is disheartening though to observe that many in need of such opportunities will not take time to assess the nature of the supposed 'work' that is involved in the opportunity. Without assessment of the opportunity, there is no possibility of discovering the gold in it. A wise man once said, if you leave your life to chance, you do not stand a chance. Chance in this saying refers to luck. Personally, I do not believe in luck. Luck is a mirage. I once heard John Maxwell say that the more you work hard at what you do, the luckier you become. I strongly believe that everyone is absolutely responsible for the outcome of his or her life.

The opportunity presented in this book might be somewhat different than what has crossed your path before; even so I am confident that just like it has changed the financial status quo of my many mentees and seminar attendees, it will not leave you on the same level financially. Of course, that is if you decide to build your gateway to success on the wings of the opportunity so presented.

Many reputable online and offline stores you celebrate today have thrived because they maximized the use of this opportunity. A lot more of them have gone ahead to build brands that are now formidable and making social impact using the ideas communicated through this book. It is not rocket science, and don't get it twisted, it is also not the ABC. It places a demand on you. It has the potential to help in the realization of your dreams and goals. It will deliver to the level of the passion with which you engage it.

Most of the important things in the world have been accomplished by people who have kept on trying when there seemed no hope at all. Thomas Edison once more put it better when he said that "Many of life's failures are people who did not realize how close they were to success when they gave up." Permit me to tweak this saying a little by saying, "Many of life's successes are people who decided to try again, one more time without the considering giving up."These categories of people are those we read about and are excited about. Theirs are the stories of grass to grace that gives us hope to try again. Perhaps this is a clarion call for you to try once again like one of my protégé, Kelvin Peters.

The bitter, biting scourge of recession in my country – Nigeria, pushed Mr. Kelvin Peters* to the doorstep of my office in 2016; he had seen my advert placement on Facebook for my Mini Importation seminar and in his dire search for a way out of his current financial mess, he showed up. Before that moment, he had fallen victim to some businesses promising geometric profit turnover. As at the time of his attendance of the seminar, he had exactly $278 in his account, and before he left my office that day, he emptied his account to sign up for my mentorship programme on Mini Importation. Months later, he confided in me that he had trekked a distance of over 3km home that day since he had no cash left at hand nor in the bank after the seminar. The trek would not bother him though; he was overjoyed at the potentially profitable business he had just learnt about.

Fast-forward to about seven months later, Kelvin now earns about $1500 to $3000 dollars monthly from his Mini Importation business. You saw that right! His monthly earning at the moment is about $1500 to $3000 and what's more?! He is poised to earning an annual income of 6 – figures from the same business this year. He keeps scaling up his business and has not relented in dreaming big to take his business to the next level.

Actually, Kelvin's case is just one of the many cases of my countrymen striving as hard as they can to get by and turn their lives around with little or no progress. An expatriate once said when he visited my country that, "opportunity for earning and becoming wealthy is so vast but the people are too blind to see it." What a comment! What an observation! This saying actually applies to many others in different countries of the world. Opportunities abound everywhere; in every part of the world. What is often missing is the opening of our eyes and knowledge of how to turn these opportunities in our favour and economic advantage. This is what this book will do for you; showing you how to achieve the financial independence you have longed for using Mini Importation as a tool.

Consumers abound in every part of the world, and purchases are made in every niche of business you can think of daily. The implication of this is that people are buying one thing or the other daily. Everyone on planet earth uses a range of products. Therefore, everyday money exchange hands from the consumer to the seller. However, many countries depend acutely on the importation of goods for their economy to thrive. Additionally, some other companies go as far as Asia – China and India – to have their manufacturing done on their behalf before eventual importation of the finished or processed product into their home country. Moreover, there are about 8 billion people in the world at the moment, which translates to billions of consumers and customers (even repeat customers) – this is the earning potential of anyone with a product to sell or offer via whatever means. The book you are holding in your hands will intimate you with one of the hottest and sweetest legitimate businesses online. Kelvin's story is just one of the many examples of people who have turned their financial status around via the use of the Mini Importation business model. You are sure to get the benign truths about starting, running and scaling up a successful Mini Importation business.

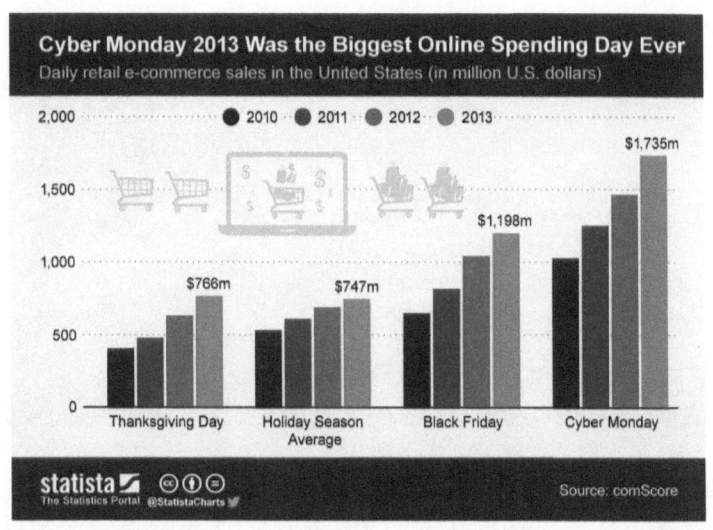

Cyber Monday 2013 Was the Biggest Online Spending Day Ever
Daily retail e-commerce sales in the United States (in million U.S. dollars)

2010 ● 2011 ● 2012 ● 2013

$1,735m

$1,198m

$766m

$747m

Thanksgiving Day | Holiday Season Average | Black Friday | Cyber Monday

statista
The Statistics Portal @StatistaCharts

Source: comScore

From the information in the picture above, the only set of people that will immensely profit from this alleged biggest online spending day in the US are the manufacturers, wholesalers and retailers. Now imagine the amount of profit that will accrue to you if you had quality products to offer. Imagine taking a share of just $250,000 from the amount expended on that day alone. Perhaps, that amount is too big for your imagination. Imagine what could have been your cut of the hundreds of millions expended on those days if you had goods to offer.

Below is another infographics showing a similar scenario.

Precisely imagine what your share would have been if you had an investment in products to retail.

This is only data for US; the same is tenable in every other country. All I am trying to do is help you see what you have been missing out on. The fact that you are not maximizing this opportunity does not mean others are not using it to their advantage.

While I was starting out in this business, there was little or no resource to read and garner necessary knowledge of the business from. I could be even considered disadvantaged because of the country I lived in. I had to learn from my bittersweet experiences, errors, mistakes and eventually from my mentors in the business. It was until I began mentoring others and raising 6 – figure annual earners from this business that I decided to expand the scope of my impact; I decided it was time to come up with a material anyone from any part of the world can use for a guide to start and build his or her own Mini Importation business. And that is what this book does exactly: the reader will not have to make the same mistakes I and countless others made and had to learn from while venturing into this business.

Having mentored hundreds of people in different parts of the world on this business model and raising several annual 6 - figure earners in the process; you can be sure of getting nothing less than an excellent guide for this business model. You will be availed the opportunity to learn from my experiences and mistakes. You will discover how to select highly profitable products for a ready market with high turnover and how to communicate directly with the manufacturers of your selected products for even better pricing on the cheap but quality products you intend to build your business upon. Also, you will learn how to watch out for common pitfalls and errors people make in the business and more importantly, how to go about niche selection.

Whether you are looking for a way to supplement your present income; looking for an entirely new stream of income or looking to start a potentially profitable business with relatively low capital at hand, then look no further; You have the answer in your hands! This is not to say that the business is not meant for those with sizable capital to invest. It sure does; it only implies more profit owing to a higher purchasing power.

One of the biggest challenges people had when starting out a business is capital. To get started in this business, however, the investment capital you need is relatively small. In fact, the investment capital is somewhat ridiculously small compared to the profit potential the opportunity avails. Therefore, there is no cause for a needless wait. You could launch your business as soon as you are through with this guide!

Among other things, the following are covered in details in this resource:

- ✓ How to easily navigate manufacturers' website.
- ✓ How to search for goods on the e-commerce sites
- ✓ How to communicate and negotiate with manufacturers directly
- ✓ How to get trusted freight forwarders
- ✓ How to pay the manufacturers/suppliers
- ✓ How to sell your products on popular e-commerce sites

✓ How to set up your own e-commerce site

As you go through the pages of this book devouring the content, I wish you will find what several hundreds of my protégé found in the course of their mentorship with me that made their lack and want a thing of the past. Personally, I am, without a shadow of doubt, assured that if you can add resilient action to the guidance provided throughout this book, then, a new level of financial independence beckons to you.

Adewale Makanjuola

2020

CHAPTER ONE

WHAT IS MINI IMPORTATION?

To start with, let us examine the concept and business of importation. Importation involves the bringing in of finished products, merchandise or commodities from abroad for use, sale or further processing by the importer. Here, shipments of goods (usually in large quantities) are delivered to the buyer (the importer) in his or her home country.

Mini importation, therefore, is the importation done on a smaller scale than nominal importation. The quantity of goods that can be imported at any particular time is as set by the manufacturer. So, in mini importation, large is a relative term. If for a product, the manufacturer has set a limit of 2 units as the smallest amount of goods that can be carted out, then 2 units become a large quantity of that particular product. The smallest amount of goods is referred to as Minimum Order Quantity (MOQ).

THE ORIGIN OF IMPORTATION

Importation is dated as far back as the production of goods and services. It has existed throughout history; for example, Uttarapatha, the popular Chinese Silk Road, Amber Road, salt roads etc. are landmarks renown for importation in history. Importation or

International Trade as some may call it purveys for any nation, the economic, social, and political importance which has been on the rise in recent centuries.

With the passage of time, importation and investment aided by technology have led to globalization. Globalization is the tendency of investment funds and businesses to move beyond domestic and national markets to other markets around the globe, allowing them to become interconnected with different markets.

Globalization is not new though. For thousands of years, people — and, later, corporations — have been buying from and selling to each other in lands at great distances, such as through the famed Silk Road across Central Asia that connected China and Europe during the Middle Ages. Likewise, for centuries, people and corporations have invested in enterprises in other countries. In fact, many of the features of the current wave of globalization are similar to those prevailing before the outbreak of the First World War in 1914.

Even so, policy and technological developments of the past few decades have spurred increases in cross-border trade, investment, and migration so large that many observers believe the world has entered a qualitatively new phase in its economic development. Since 1950, for example, the volume of world trade has increased by 20 times, and from just 1997 to 1999 flows of foreign investment nearly doubled, from $468 billion to $827 billion.

Technology, as a facilitator of importation, has been the other principal driver of globalization. Advances in information technology, in particular, have dramatically transformed economic life. Information technologies have given all sorts of individual economic actors — consumers, investors, startups, businesses — valuable new tools for identifying and pursuing economic opportunities, including faster and more informed analyses of economic trends around the world, easy transfers of assets, and collaboration with far–flung partners.

KEY COUNTRIES TO CONSIDER

You cannot have bread without flour; cake without eggs; ham without pig; neither can you talk about importation without mentioning some countries. Some of these countries include; United States of America, Japan, China, Germany, France, Korea, United Kingdom, Italy, Netherlands, etc. to name a few. These countries have been major contributors to globalization. They have annually churned out metric tonnes of goods that have contributed to the global economy.

Consider the following statistics represented in the tables and charts below:

Rank	Country	Exports (million $)	Date of information	% of GDP [2]
-	world	$ 17,979,000 [3]	2014 is.	29.5
-	European Union (excluding intra-EU trade)	$ 2,659,000 [3]	2016 is.	
1	china	$ 2,011,000 [1]	2016 is	22.1
2	United States	$ 1,471,000	2016 is.	12.6
3	germany	$ 1,283,000 [3]	2016 is.	46.8
4	japan	$ 641,400 [3]	2016 is.	17.9
5	South Korea	$ 509,000 [3]	2016 is.	45.9
6	la France	$ 505,400 [3]	2016 is.	30.0
7	Hong Kong	$ 487,700 [3]	2016 is.	201.6
8	Netherlands	$ 460,100 [3]	2016 is.	82.5
9	italy	$ 436,300 [3]	2016 is.	30.1
10	United Kingdom	$ 412,100 [3]	2016 is.	27.2

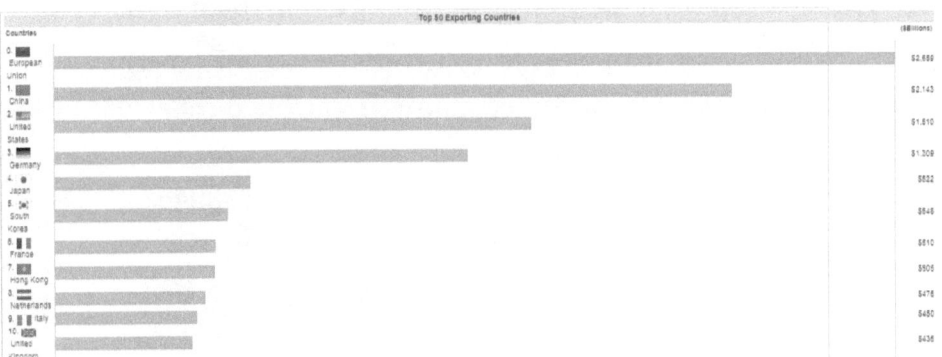

From the table and the graph, you will observe that the United States and China are the two leading nations that export the most. In addition, for years now, China has been the most competitive manufacturing nation

14

compared to the US. Germany, on the other hand, has held firm the third position for decades now.

A quick overview of manufacturing facts of US and China is highlighted below:

- **In the most recent data, manufacturers contributed $2.18 trillion to the US economy in 2016.** This figure has risen since the second quarter of 2009, when manufacturers contributed $1.70 trillion. Over that same time frame, value-added output from durable goods manufacturing grew from $0.87 trillion to $1.20 trillion, with nondurable goods output up from $0.85 trillion to $1.00 trillion. In 2016, manufacturing accounted for 11.7 percent of GDP in the economy. (Source: Bureau of Economic Analysis)

- **Over the past 25 years, US – manufactured goods exports have quadrupled.** In 1990, for example, US manufacturers exported $329.5 billion in goods. By 2000, that number had more than doubled to $708.0 billion. In 2014, it reached an all-time high, for the fifth consecutive year, of $1.403 trillion, despite slowing global growth. With that said, a number of economic headwinds have dampened export demand since then, with US – manufactured goods exports down 6.1 percent in 2015 to $1.317 trillion. (Source: US Commerce Department)

- **Taken alone, manufacturing in the United States would be the ninth-largest economy in the world.** With $2.1 trillion in value added from manufacturing in 2014, only eight other nations (including the US) would rank higher in terms of their gross domestic product.Source: Bureau of Economic Analysis, International Monetary Fund)

Some facts about the manufacturing industry in China include:

- China is the largest workforce for manufacturing with over 115 million workers
- More than 75 percent worlds umbrellas were made in China
- Out of 500 companies, more than 400 companies are investing in the manufacturing in China.
- China manufactures more than 70% of all the mobile phones sold worldwide.
- China produces more than 90% of the world's personal computers.

- China produces more than 60% pair of shoes in the world.
- China's tea production accounts for 33 percent of the world's total.

This is to highlight but a few. The list of relevant facts for both countries' manufacturing power is not exhaustive.

After many years of competitive manufacturing with the United States of America, by 2010, China became the largest manufacturing economy in the world (with a 23.2% share of manufacturing activity) through extremely fast growth in the physical volume of value–added and modest inflation. The US is in second place with a 17.2% share. China has more than four times the population of the United States, and through its manufacturing intensity of $1,978 per capita value-added in 2013 is high for a developing economy, it is well behind advanced countries such as the United States ($6, 338).

China widened the lead it had over the US and since then, just as was portrayed in the table and graph shown above; China still leads the US in manufacturing and global goods export.

Data as at 2013:

Rank	% of World Manufacturing 2013	2013	Valued in U.S. Dollars 2003	1993
1	23.2%	China	United States	United States
2	17.2%	United States	Japan	Japan
3	7.8%	Japan	China	Germany
4	6.3%	Germany	Germany	China
5	3.1%	Korea	Italy	France
6	2.4%	Italy	France	Italy
7	2.4%	France	United Kingdom	United Kingdom
8	2.3%	Russia	Korea	Brazil
9	2.1%	Brazil	Canada	Russia
10	2.0%	United Kingdom	Spain	Korea
11	2.0%	India	Mexico	Spain
12	1.8%	Mexico	Africa	Canada
13	1.7%	Indonesia	Brazil	Mexico
14	1.6%	Canada	India	Turkey
15	1.4%	Spain	Netherlands	Netherlands

INTERNET: THE GAME CHANGER FOR IMPORTATION

Before the advent of the internet, a lot of stress was associated with the importation business. It was just like another job owned by an entrepreneur with no benefit of time freedom; freedom from the attendant stress of going to the country of import to procure goods and settling the logistics of bringing it into the home country of the importer. The norm was to go outside one's home country to import goods. This causes a whole lot of stress on the part of the importer and is capital intensive. What of the financial risks this poses? Many custom officers have turned this to their own major way of extorting money from importers. In their bid to ensure the adherence to the terms of the trade agreement between the country of import and export, they exploit importers, forcing them to pay unprecedented amounts aside the statutory tariff imposed by the trade agreement.

Although the importer still manages to make an appreciable profit from the importation business this way, the toll it is taking on his health; togetherness and control of his life are not endearing. I believe this is one of the reasons why people would scarcely consider delving into the mini importation business. There has been a mindset of profit through the gloom, blood, and sweat ascribed to the importation business by observers from afar off. A few years ago this might have been true, but not anymore. This has changed all thanks to the rapid development of technology.

As an importer, on a normal business day; you will have to book and pay for flight to visit the country of import; go locate customers to buy from; get the right category of goods; pay hotel fees and bills for your accommodation all the while you are in that country and accrue expenses on many other logistics that are actually time and energy demanding. But with mini importation, you do this comfortably. You erase the accompanying stress that comes with actually traveling to these countries to import; all these are now made possible courtesy of the relentless drive at technology development and the power of the internet.

With the availability of the internet, over time, the attendant stress that comes with importation was soon to become a thing of the past. It became possible to connect via emails and websites owned by the manufacturers/suppliers of the imported products. Plus, a lot of money was being saved by this new method thus making way for increased earning potential to the importer.

Early last year, a lady visited my office to celebrate with me on my wedding anniversary. She told me that she is an interior decorator; that she also sells decorating materials and accessories to people in her line of vocation. She said she has been traveling to Dubai on several occasions to buy materials for her work; bring it to Nigeria and then sell. However, she learned through one of my seminars about a particular e-commerce website where she could actually get 'anything' she wanted.

Without delay, she took it as a challenge. She visited the website and searched for the decorating materials she had aforetime been traveling to Dubai to get. She was amazed when she saw these items in their various types, varieties, and colours at a very cheap price. She could not keep mum; these are the things she actually leaves Nigeria to go get in Dubai. She has had to pay for flight ticket; go through daunting stress navigating the market to get her desired stock in Dubai and then come back to Nigeria to calculate her expenses in order to determine a befitting selling price which now will be on the high side for her to make a profit.

This was a whole new experience for her. At a sitting, she found all these things online and at a cheaper price. Now she is fully into the mini importation of the same products, and she is making an awesome profit from it in a more relaxed fashion. When she told me this, I was so joyous and glad that someone is actually making use of something I taught to her advantage and positive difference; she is making sense of the whole thing, and it is helping her career and business.

Mind you, even though she now gets the same décor materials at a cheaper price from **'my ultimate e-commerce site'** she still sells it at the former price she was retailing before discovering the site. In fact, when other merchants were adding more to the cost of the materials, she joined them to place a slight increment on the prices of her stock. After all, not everyone needs to know her secret.

Take a look at the products below and make a guess of their prices:

From left to right; based on your experience purchasing online, the prices you might have guessed for the black gown, the deep blue top, and shoe below will go something like $20, $40 and $30 right?

I may not have perfectly second-guessed you, but I know I am close.

Let me now give you a shocker:

The shoe costs $5.7;

The black gown costs $5.8 and

The deep blue gown costs $4.44.

I believe I got your attention now. Read on and be flabbergasted.

Just for emphasis, in case you are wondering how ridiculous those prices are, the internet is the deal breaker for conventional importation. With a laptop and an internet connection, from any part of the world, you can communicate with a manufacturer of a product you want to purchase and have your goods brought to you in your country. This is one of the things that make mini importation so magical. A lot of the attendant stress with the conventional importation has been eliminated; the cost of starting up the business is drastically reduced and the potential of scaling up businesses is greatly increased.

More so, with the continuous rise of e-commerce websites that offer products to the end consumers directly from the manufacturer's stable, your work as a mini importer has been made relatively easy. You at this moment shop as though you were purchasing groceries from a store online only that in this case, you are shopping to make a profit via retail or wholesale to retailers.

Mini importation is such a business that when you go into it; you do not really need a huge capital. All you need is a proper guide with the right idea and a little capital to kick-start your business. You can kick-start a successful mini importation business with less than $55 or a maximum of $55 and before you know it; you would be making a huge profit; double or more of your investment capital. You can turn your initial of $55 into hundreds or thousands of dollars and with continuous investment and relentless scaling of your business, it can become millions of dollars. Whatever your financial goals are; I am confident this business can help you reach it and even go beyond.

WHY OPT FOR MINI IMPORTATION?
- **HIGH PROFITABILITY**

Many of the goods sold in your local community and several other popular online stores in various nations of the world are perceived by consumers as being sold for a fair price (but for the exception of some obvious few ones). It is widely accepted that making money or making profits is achieved by either selling goods or providing services. In mini importation, you are selling both goods and services and that is exactly what you will be paid for. Your role in this business is to provide goods that an ever–demanding market of consumers are looking to lay their hands upon to meet a need. Your profit is inherent in the place of procurement of the goods you are selling and the price for which you were able to purchase the products and of course, the price at which you were able to sell it to your customers. Definitely, the cheaper you are able to get the products you are dealing, the higher your profit potential.

However, the frank truth is that most of the goods you come across in online stores and in real life marketplaces and malls are being sold at exorbitant prices. Some are being sold at three times the cost at which the goods were procured. And this is the opportunity being explored by everyone involved in the mini importation business.

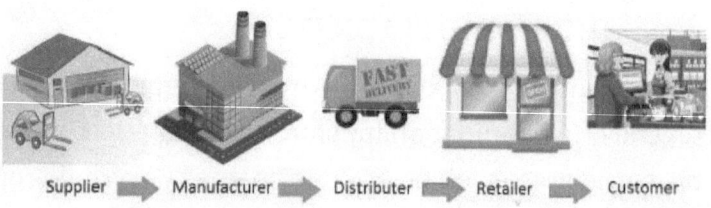

Supplier ➡ Manufacturer ➡ Distributer ➡ Retailer ➡ Customer

The picture above shows a typical supply chain from the supplier to the end consumer. What I want to achieve here is to help you have a good understanding of your channel(s) of profiting in this business. At every juncture of the supply chain, everyone adds a profit to the product and the consequence of this is that the final price of the product becomes relatively high at the point of purchase when it eventually gets to the final consumer.

For instance, the cost of producing the wristwatch shown below is less than $5; from the manufacturer/supplier has to make a profit, he gives it to the importer at $5. The wholesaler/importer then sells it to a small business owner at $10. Also, for profit maximization, the small business owner sells to the consumer (a retailer) at $15. In this case you are the small business owner buying from the 'big' importer and your own profit is just $5 per wristwatch sold.

What startles me is that most end consumers will end up buying this same wristwatch at a price higher than $15, yet they will still deem the product 'cheap' and affordable. Anyway, this is what the mini importer uses for his or her advantage.

Before...

1 — Watch Factory in China

2 — Big Importer

3 — Small Business

Factory sells to Big Importer at wholesale price of $5 per watch

Big importer sells to YOU (Small Business) at higher price of $10 per watch

You finally sell the watch to a customer for $15

Your profit is only $5

Let us now consider how a mini importer makes a cool profit from this same supply chain:

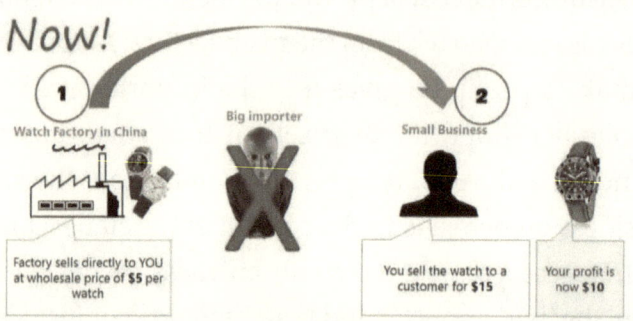

When you decide to go into mini importation, you eliminate the need for a wholesaler: You connect directly with the manufacturer; order for the wristwatch which the manufacturer will give to you at the same fair price of $5. By so doing you will be saving $5 for every unit of wristwatch you are buying (you were losing this to the big importer before). In spite of this, you will still be selling to your retailers at $15; making you a profit of $10 per unit of wristwatch sold instead of the initial $5 you made using the previous model.

Now imagine going on a little further to personally retail the wristwatches. Yes! It is possible. Many mini importers are doing it and this amounts to even higher profit. Assuming the street market price for the wristwatch is $22, the profit of the mini importer amounts to $17 on every unit of the wristwatch he sells. This is ridiculous but real; uncapped profit potential at the behest of every mini importer.

The money that ought to be added by the wholesaler (and by the retailer in some cases as I have exemplified) will become yours.

- **A READY MARKET AWAITS YOU**

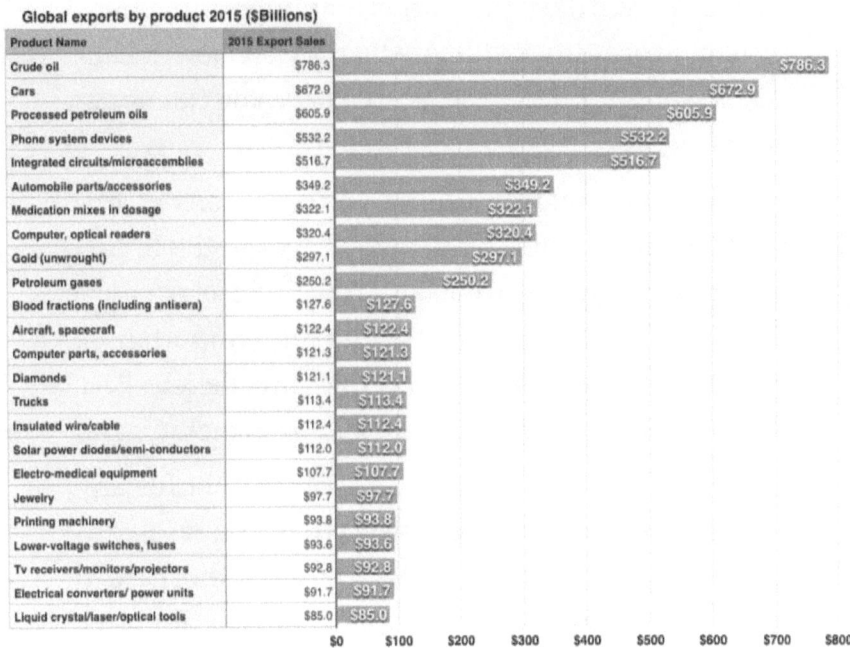

Global exports by product 2015 ($Billions)

Product Name	2015 Export Sales
Crude oil	$786.3
Cars	$672.9
Processed petroleum oils	$605.9
Phone system devices	$532.2
Integrated circuits/microassemblies	$516.7
Automobile parts/accessories	$349.2
Medication mixes in dosage	$322.1
Computer, optical readers	$320.4
Gold (unwrought)	$297.1
Petroleum gases	$250.2
Blood fractions (including antisera)	$127.6
Aircraft, spacecraft	$122.4
Computer parts, accessories	$121.3
Diamonds	$121.1
Trucks	$113.4
Insulated wire/cable	$112.4
Solar power diodes/semi-conductors	$112.0
Electro-medical equipment	$107.7
Jewelry	$97.7
Printing machinery	$93.8
Lower-voltage switches, fuses	$93.6
Tv receivers/monitors/projectors	$92.8
Electrical converters/ power units	$91.7
Liquid crystal/laser/optical tools	$85.0

Exports made in the 24 product categories listed above amounts to a total of $6.15trillion. That is a whole lot of money flying around in importation and exportation of several billions of goods in all the 24 categories listed in the infographic above.

May I ask this: Of the jewellery market valued at approximately $100billion, how much have you made from it? Almost everyone on planet Earth uses a mobile phone today; in fact, the market for phones and phone system devices is worth more than $530billion dollars; yet, how much of this gigantic sum have you claimed as yours?

I could go on and on asking you questions of this template all in a bid to open your eyes to the billion dollar market ready to consume the diverse products you could deal when you are into mini importation. Imagine what 0.0001% of the $97.7billion of the jewellery product category will do to your finances at the moment.

The bottom line is, there is a ready market for any product niche you decide to deal when you resolve to own a mini importation business. You would not need to start a frantic search for the consumer of your products. They already exist; they are hungrily waiting to pay you for what you want to bring to the table.

THE DEMANDS OF THE BUSINESS

The story was told about an aid group in South Africa. They once wrote to a missionary, David Livingstone asking, "Have you found a good road to where you are? If so, we want to know how to send other men to join you."

In response, Livingstone said, "If you have men who will come only if they know there is a good road, I do not want them. I want men who will come even if there is no road at all." This is the kind of resolve that is expected of anyone that wants to go all in into mini importation.

To attain your level of desired success in this business, you must be ready to do what others are not ready to. To pay the price many are unwilling to pay and sacrifice much in return for the attainment of your goals. Nothing of worth comes easy in life. Let this truth always guide your step. I may have found a way to guide you through setting up a highly successful mini importation business, yet; you have to be dogged at your approach to making something out of it.

For you to make anything meaningful out of your mini importation business, you need to count the cost and be ready to pay the price. Taken, it is assured that the business model is a highly profitable one with a reduced stress level; nevertheless, this is not a cause for mental laxity on the part of whoever desires to start this business.

In no particular order, the following are the demands of the business:

- **CONTINUOUS RESEARCH AND LEARNING**

Nothing is static. The only constant thing in life is a change. It has been found that the volume of information accessible so far since the 20th century began is greater than all the information available accessed in the 17th, 18th, and 19th century combined.

Top-performing business owners know there is no "secret" to success, but rather a tireless commitment to working hard everyday to keep both customers satisfied and happy. The old adage "you get out of it what you put into it" is often repeated for a good reason. In any vocation, achieving and maintaining success means a constant investment of time, money and energy. Nothing delivers beyond the level of passion, and commitment invested in it.

One way businessmen stay at the top of their game in mini importation is by continuing to invest in market research. The best, most successful mini importers go the extra mile to carry out an effective market research. Don't be naïve; this process doesn't occur only in large companies with many employees and a large budget. You as a small business owner, starting out in the mini importation business will also need market research and the only difference is in dimension and quantity of the markets that will be analyzed because large companies have markets with larger dimension and quantity than small businesses.

Market research will allow you to learn more about past, current and potential customers and with that understanding, you can make better decisions related to satisfying their needs from which your immense profiting will come rolling.

Here are some benefits of market research:

- ✓ Excellent market research and quality decision making based on facts received from marketing research will ensure the survival of your business in the market.
- ✓ With quality market research, you can identify opportunities for your business and at the same time will prevent threats that will come from the market.
- ✓ You will always know and constantly will learn about your customers, your competitors and your marketing
- ✓ You can easily succeed in lowering risks about new products or services that you plan to

introduce on a specific market because these products and services will be arranged for the real market demand.

✓ This process will give you all basic marketing benchmarks that you must complete. In such a way, you can evaluate your marketing efforts and constantly improve the overall marketing

There can be no over emphasizing how vital continuous research and learning is in this venture. There is a need for you to always timely review hot selling products; ready markets for a particular product; engage in a tireless and relentless search for websites where products can be purchased at a very cheap price and connect with other successful mini importers making waves in the business.

Concisely, when you devote your time, energy and resources to continuous improvement your business will witness immeasurable benefits, including:

- Increased productivity
- Improved quality of services
- Lowered costs
- Decreased delivery times
- Improved customer satisfaction
- Reduced product return rate

- **HAVE 'SMART' GOALS & PLAN**

Many have wished their way to their present quagmire. Wishes do not avail anything; only goals do. According to Brian Tracy, "a goal is something distinctly different from a wish. It is clear, written, and specific. It can be quickly and easily described to another person. You can measure it, and you know when you have achieved it or not." So, do away with your mediocre and failure mentality. Your problem is to bridge the gap between where you are now and the goals you intend to reach.

Goals are practical steps, measured steps, definite steps and realistic steps mapped out to achieve desired results. They are units of actions into which your business objectives are broken into to become manageable units to enable you to accomplish the whole. Your goals are action steps that birth proofs noiselessly when accomplished.

Your goals must be clearly defined before you go about this business, and you must have a **'SMART'** plan as a wheel to take you there. Any business that does not have a **SMART** goal and a plan to see it to fruition is bound to fail. In fact, this is one of the commonest reasons why businesses, especially startups, fail. You cannot just go into this business without knowing what you are doing.

You need to have **SMART** goals with a tandem plan. **SMART** is a mnemonic device for:

S – SPECIFIC

M – MEASURABLE

A – ACHIEVABLE

R – REALISTIC

T – TIME BOUND

You may have seen this before and even know what the letters represent but have you always applied it to make it work for you? This is actually very important; setting SMART goals is a smart move; it can change the outlook of your business or any vocation you lay your hands upon.

S - SPECIFIC

Focus is key! If you chase two rabbits, both will escape. Hellen Keller said, "I am only one: but I am still one. I cannot do everything, but still, I can do something; I will not refuse to do something I can do." Only men of focus make headway in life. It has been the guiding principle of the greatest businessmen of our time like Richard Branson, Jack Welsh, Warren Buffet and many more. If it worked for them, you can be sure it will work for you.

Your productivity is inherent in your focus. The results you command in this business are in direct proportion to how much of yourself you devoted to running this business. Have you not heard? Feed your focus and starve your distractions, they say.

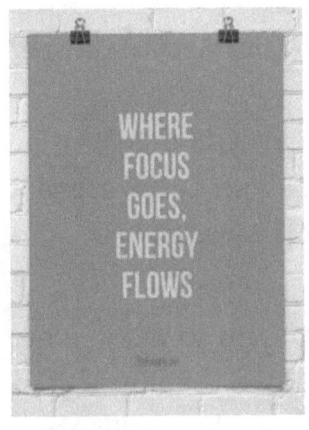

WHERE FOCUS GOES, ENERGY FLOWS

How does this apply to you and the business of mini importation you may ask? Being **specific** about the product connotes the fact that you must spell out the goods you want to buy and start dealing. You cannot go into all the goods listed on the sites you come across. I'm sure with the array and quality of products you see on these e-commerce sites, you might be tempted to deal in a number of products. Nonetheless, you have to pick a niche. FOCUS – Follow One Course Until Successful.

Have a niche. If you want to go into women clothing, then focus on the women's clothing line only. If it is men's clothing category, then go for it. In settling for a niche to deal, the following are the questions you sincerely need to ask: Can I sell it? Are people ready to buy it?

Other things you must spell out clearly as you decide to go about this business include:

- When am I starting the business?
- When am I to expect my orders?
- What channels am I employing to sell my products?
- For how much am I selling my merchandise per unit?
- How much profit am I expecting?
- When do I expect to have both my investment capital and profit in my possession?
- When am I placing my next order?

Go further, think and come up with so many other things that will enhance the smooth running of your business. Then take bold giant steps to be specific about them.

Do not assume any of these. Without focusing and getting to clarity, you cannot lead; you cannot motivate; you cannot plan; you cannot communicate, and you cannot make significant progress in this business.

Be specific at every juncture of your business. This is the way to go. This is the way to thrive.

M – MEASURABLE

Your business plans must be quantifiable in dates and timelines. There must be a way for you to gauge your progress.

Include precise amounts, dates, and so on in your goals so you can measure your degree of success. If your goal is simply defined as "To make a profit" how will you know when you have become successful? In one month's time if you have a 1 percent increment in your income or in two years' time when you have a 10 percent increment?

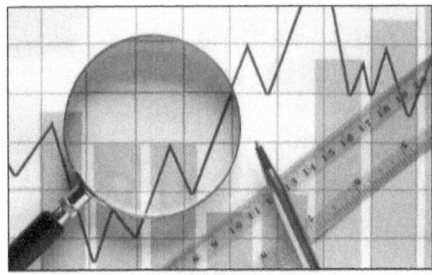 Without a way to measure your success you miss out on the celebration that comes with knowing you have actually achieved something. More importantly, you will be cast aside on the scheme of things in your business generally. This goes ahead to corroborate the initial point we discussed – about being specific.

Clarity is of the essence. Any plans and goals you set that cannot be split into timelines are questionable. It is a precursor to not achieving the set goal. Besides, having a measurable goal is an inherent control method for your plans. It helps you to assess the level of your progress towards your goal per time.

Still on clarity; establish concrete criteria for evaluating your progress toward the attainment of each goal you set.

When you measure your progress, you stay on track, reach your target dates, and experience the exhilaration of achievement that spurs you on to continued efforts required to reach your goal.

A - ATTAINABLE

Your plans must be such that they make your goals reachable. It means it must be real, accurate and able to be accomplished. It is not something you cook up because of a little urge or momentary impulse.

You must be sure that you can attain your business goals and plans. Since you will be investing your hard-earned money into the business; it is only wise to sit down and ask if it is promising to attain your goals.

 Make sure that it's possible to achieve the goals you set. If you set a goal that you have no hope of achieving, you will simply demoralize yourself and erode your confidence. Your morale will go down at the speed of light.

However, resist the urge to set goals that are too easy. They will not challenge you. Accomplishing a goal that you didn't have to work hard for can cause you disappointment at best, and can also make you fear setting future goals that carry a risk of non-achievement.

By setting realistic yet challenging goals, you hit the balance you need. These are the types of goals that require you to "raise the bar" and they bring the greatest personal satisfaction.

R – RELEVANT

Seeing the potential of this business, many go ahead to imagine wild about the kind of profit they expect to make. To make matters worse, they have heard the rags-to-riches stories of others and are fired up to replicate same in their lives. This pushes them to make a brutal mistake; they set an unrealistic business goal for themselves.

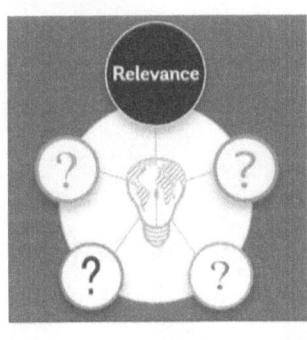

The truth is, I believe your income potential in this business is uncapped; it is limitless. However, I also believe inconsistent progress. In fact, this is the part of their stories these testifiers do not tell and emphasize.

On your part, your goals should not all be about money. Entrepreneurship is not about garnering money. It is about value creation and addition. Whatever goals you are setting and plans you are forging to make it happen must align with this purpose.

Your goals should be relevant to the direction you want your business to take. By keeping goals aligned with this, you will develop the focus you need to get ahead and do what you want. Set widely scattered and inconsistent goals, and you'll fritter your time – and your resources – away.

T – TIME BOUND

Almost everything revolves around time. For example, you must know when your goods will arrive; you must have a time range for selling off the products and going back to update your  stock. If this business is not time bound you will notice that you will have goods on hand that you have forgotten about gathering dust somewhere in your store or closet.

Give yourself a target: My products must come in within so and so time; I want to sell it within so and so period; I must have sold it by this date; I want to have made all my sales and gathered all my capital, my profit and have my turnover at hand. So, it must time bound!

Your goals must have a deadline. The implication of this is that you know when you can celebrate success. When you are working against a deadline, your sense of urgency increases and achievement will come that much quicker.

By now, it is my hope that you are revved up to explore and make a turnaround for the better in finances riding on the wings of mini importation. I, therefore, suffice it to say, welcome to the world of importation. Welcome to Mini Importation.

Without much ado, let us explore the amazing websites that avail you stress-free, ridiculous profit-making importation.

CHAPTER 2

OVERVIEW OF SELECTED E-COMMERCE SITES

One of the major reasons why I took up the challenge to start teaching and mentoring people about mini importation is to reduce the number of people going through financial hardship. It became more pressing to do so be when my country – Nigeria, went into a long period of recession. Different get–rich–quick schemes were springing up and millions of people were falling victim of these malicious Ponzi schemes. A lot of people were desperate for an additional means of income to supplement their current earnings. Many were seeking ways to increase their income and meet their needs as an individual and/or a family. I knew I had to step in to offer this solution that I have proven to work over time. However, I have always had to quell the mentality that mini importation is a stressful, capital intensive business in the minds of the majority of the prospects that attended my way.

There are yet some people who think because of the high exchange rate now, they will spend more on starting their business owing to the cost of bringing the goods to their country. However, the truth remains that this business is one you go into, investing a relatively low capital and have no cause for regret afterward. You're profiting is unquestionable given the right guidance and directive.

For price comparison, I have decided to showcase some women dresses, men shoes and sneakers, chokers and baby bottle from the renowned Amazon. The purpose is to help you vividly see what is obtainable through similar popular e-commerce sites where people shop compared with the e-commerce sites I will be unveiling in this chapter. With a focus on the prices of these items, I am sure you will acquiesce that you have before now spent *wastefully* on some items you buy online. In fact, you have always enriched the sellers of these products on the popular e-commerce sites you buy from.

Beautiful dresses at ridiculous retail prices; the lowest amongst them costs $79.50

Women's Honeycomb Stripe Dress
$119⁵⁰ prime

Women's Stripe Flare Sleeve Dress
$129⁵⁰ prime

Women's Alayiah Lace Velvet Flutter Sle...
$79⁵⁰ prime

Women's renae Ruffle Peplum Mini Dress
$99⁵⁰ prime

Kearia Womens Sexy Black
Sequin Scoop Neck Long Sleeve
Bodycon Party Midi Dress
$24.99 - $25.99 √prime
★★★☆☆ ▾ 147

HOMEYEE Women's Chic V-Neck
Lace Patchwork Flare Party Dress
A062
$34.99 - $38.99 √prime
★★★★☆ ▾ 33

AlvaQ Women's Sexy V Neck Off
The Shoulder Evening Bodycon
Club Midi Dress
$19.99 √prime
★★★★☆ ▾ 1,159

Ebbizt Womens Off The Shoulder
High Low Bodycon Mermaid
Evening Party Midi Dress
$19.99 √prime
★★★★☆ ▾ 25

These are party dresses: the lowest priced among goes for a whopping sum of $20. Now let us take a look at the jewellery category – chokers:

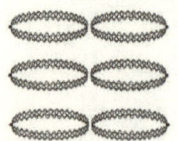

Mudder 6 Pieces Black Tattoo
Choker Necklace Stretch Gothic
Tattoo Henna Elastic Choker
Necklace Set
$6.09 √prime
★★★★☆ ▾ 91

Daycindy Bar Pendant Coin Chain
Multi Layer Choker Necklace for
Women, 13" Silver and Golden
$7.88 √prime
★★★★☆ ▾ 72

Black Choker Set, Outee 9 Pcs
Black Velvet Choker Necklace
Velvet Kids Black Choker
Necklace Tattoos Velvet Choker...
$6.99 √prime
★★★★☆ ▾ 511

Outee 30 PCS Black Velvet
Choker Necklace Set Henna
Tattoo Choker Set Velvet Tattoo
Ribbon Velvet Choker Set for...
$10.99 √prime
★★★★☆ ▾ 118

This may not seem outrageous to you at the moment, but later in the book, I will unveil a site where the most expensive of these chokers, priced $11 costs way less than $2. This of course implies that none of the four chokers displayed above cost exactly $2.

To paint to you a more graphic picture, imagine you had to buy all four chokers displayed above. At the stipulated prices on Amazon, the total cost of them all will be:

$$\$6.09 + \$7.88 + \$6.99 + +10.99 = \$39.15$$

The total cost of procuring all the displayed chokers is $39.15. This is such an absurd price.

Now, imagine we bought it from the site I am soon to show you at $2 each; that is a total cost of $8 for the exact same kinds of chokers. By so doing you will have saved:

$$\$39.15 - \$8 = \$23.95$$

$23.95 dollars is a sizeable amount of money to be saved. I hope you agree with me on that. Well, that is exactly how you also will profit from this business. All businesses prey on the seeming ignorance of the consumers. The truth is that most consumers still find the prices of these products available on Amazon 'cheap'. And that is what makes for the profiting of mini importers like me and soon to be, you.

Although the list of products to be used for price comparison is not exhaustive; let us look into a few more categories of products – jewellery, men, and babies.

If your guess at the moment is that I will quip that "there are sites that offer the above products at lesser prices," then you are correct.

I want you to trust me when I say that all the products I have hitherto shown to you are expensive. They are priced way too expensively.

You may even want to empathize with the seller; considering the cost of production/importation, shipping fees and all, it still does not negate the clear fact that all these products are expensive.

Men's 1948 Mid Sneaker
from $ 37⁵⁵ prime
★★★☆☆ ▾ 4

BOSS Green by Hugo Boss Men's Enligh...
from $ 258²³ prime

Men's Mason Brushed Leather Sneaker
from $ 64¹⁹ prime

Men's Soft 7 Woven Slip On Fashion Sn...
$ 169⁹⁵ prime
★★★☆☆ ▾ 1

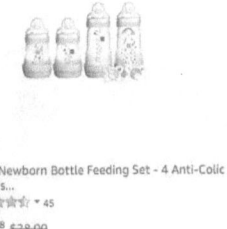

MAM Newborn Bottle Feeding Set - 4 Anti-Colic
Bottles...
★★★★☆ ▾ 45
$ 17⁸⁸ $28.00
 prime
FREE Shipping on eligible orders

Not to worry though, the same way others are profiting from this kind of pricing on their goods unhindered, so will you. You will also be taking advantage of this to become cash rich and perhaps debt free; your finances will take an upward turn.

Without further fuss, below is a list of e-commerce sites where products that cut across diverse categories can be obtained. Upon visiting the site, you will surely come across amazing pictures and might feel the urge to go in for as many product categories that catch your eye, do not fall for that. Remember, you have to settle for a niche; not based on what you like or how admirable the pictures you see on these sites are but based on your sincere evaluation on the ease with which you can sell the products and the availability of a ready market to consume the products.

1. # WWW.599FASHION.COM

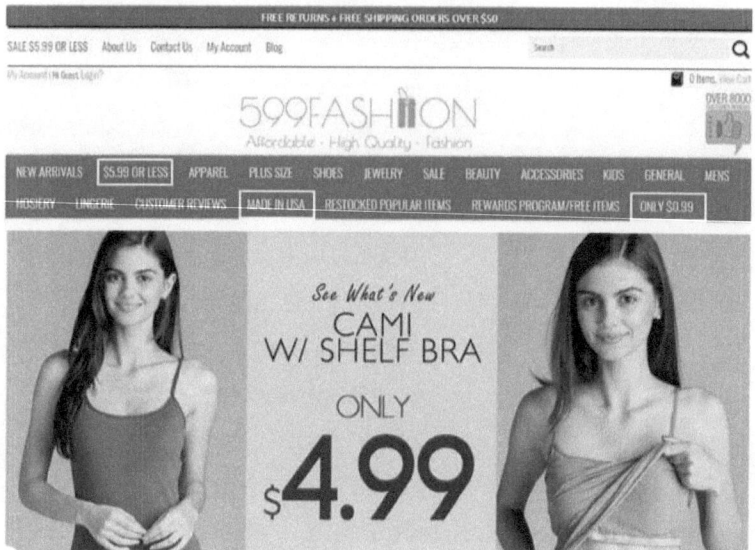

As you can see, the following product categories exist on the site:

* Apparel

* Plus Size

* Shoes

* Accessories

* Kids

* Lingerie

* $1 items

* Hosiery

599fashion.com is a US e-commerce website. The site boasts of over 3,500 items that are $5.99 or less. From my experience using this site, they have lovely fashion items which are truly either slightly lower than $5.99 or a little higher than $5.99. However, some products on the site cost way more than $5.99 and may not be advisable for you to deal in your business except you have clients that will afford the merchandise at an expensive price whenever you take delivery of the items.

For the apparel category, the site caters satisfactorily well for tops, dresses, basic wears, sleepwear, bottoms, socks and underwear, swimwear, outerwear, jumpsuit and rompers, and active wears for various occasions. The wonderful thing is that all the items in the apparel category are also available for people of plus sizes.

What of shoes? 599fashion.com is a go-to for quality sandals, heels, flats, wedges, sneakers, boots, and slippers. You will be wrong to think they cater exclusively for female only; they also have cool fashion items for men.

For the jewellery category, you will find listed on the site, diverse earrings, bracelets, necklaces, rings and sets of jewellery. Even though thousands of products are available under this category, you may not find some specific items you desire e.g. chokers.

This does not mean that the site is relatively unprofitable to work with. In fact, in just one click on the site, you could get an array of high-quality goods worth, specifically $1, $2, $3, $4, $5 and $6. And as though you cannot get enough from this site, there is an avenue for you to avail yourself clearance sales from 599fashion. It is something to look forward to and timely participate in for profit maximization.

One tricky category of products on the site that people seldom explore is the Accessories category. Many assume it includes only fashion category. This is not so. In this category, you could get belts, handbags, hats, phone accessories, key chain, sunglasses, scarves and hair accessories.

Kids are also not left out on the goodies the site has to offer. You will find items for boys and girls here. They, however, do not have as many stocks for this category as you might be expecting to find.

One of the highlights of this site is the availability of Made in USA products and Restocked Popular Items. I advise you to carefully explore this category to your advantage. There is also a Rewards Program to their loyal customers of which you soon are to become one.

As is required of a good e-commerce site, 599fashion has a provision for customer reviews. This avails you the opportunity to learn from previous experiences of customers on the site. One endearing thing about the site is the relative ease of site navigation they have in place. To crown it all up, their customer service provision is effective and makes for easy communication and guide while using the site.

2.   WWW.LOVELYWHOLESALE.COM

It is often said of lovelywholesale.com that they have an affordable item for every hobby and lifestyle. How true this is! The following are the categories and subcategories of products you can find on lovelywholesale.com:

- Dresses

  Mini Dresses, Maxi Dresses, Print Dresses, Long Sleeve Dresses, Sexy Dresses, Casual Dresses, Lace Dresses and Cocktail Dresses

- Jumpsuits

  Bodysuits, Skinny jumpsuits, Rompers, Long Sleeve jumpsuits, Plus – size jumpsuits

- Two Pieces

  Tracksuits, Two-piece Dress, Two-piece jumpsuits, Long Sleeve two pieces

- Tops

  Blouses and Shirts, Sweaters & Cardigans, Sweats & Hoodies, Camisole & Tank Tops, Long Sleeve Tops

- Bottoms

  Jeans, Leggings, Pants, Shorts, Wide Leg, Skirts, Hole/Ripped Jeans, Pants

- Swimwear

  Bikinis, Tankini, Print bikinis, One piece, Cover-ups, Three pieces

- Outwear & Coats

  Coat & Jacket, Blazer & Suits, Down & Parkas, Wool & Blends, Trench Coats, Vests & Waist Coats

- Accessories

  Jewellery, Scarves & Hats, Sexy Lingerie, Bags, Sunglasses.

As you may have observed, if you are exclusively into men clothes and fashion, then lovelywholesale.com is not the site for you.

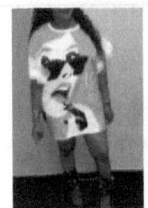

Fashionable Round Neck Printed Pink Polyester Mini
USD 10.49

Leisure Hooded Collar Long Sleeves Hollow-out Blac
USD 10.49

Euramerican Long Sleeves Brown Cotton Blend Mini D
USD 10.49

Casual Hooded Collar Hollow-out Grey Polyester Mid
USD 10.49

While many have complained about the quality of the pictures of products on this site, I want you to know that it is immaterial. The products from lovelywholesale.com are wonderful at best and will fetch you good profit and a lot of customer appreciation. The quality of the products is amazing. The items available on the site are elegant, funky and classy.

If your market audience is a partying one, you are about to make loads of money from here dealing top stylish items. You will be wowed when you actually check out this site for yourself.

With over 3 million followers on Facebook, lovelywholesale.com is the last resort for millions of people when quality and affordable fashion items come to mind. It is important to note that on this site fashion items cost about $9 – $12. It is also a US e-commerce website.

Lovelywholesale.com offers excellent, comprehensive customer service every step along the way. Before you order, you could make real time inquiries through the use of the site's live chat. Once you've made a purchase, their customer service representatives are always on-hand to answer questions through the website.

3.   WWW.OVERSTOCK.COM

Perhaps you know some people whose longings are often for expensive quality items. Many are conscious of the prices of their clothes, shoes, fashion accessories and other things they use. They do this at times not for a show, but as a representation of their personality. In fact, they have developed a knack for recognizing quality. The amazing thing about this set of people is that they can afford these high-priced products and will spare no expense to acquire them once it appeals to their taste. If you have such clients, then overstock.com is the site you need to satisfy their thirst for quality and cost.

You could shop by department as shown below;

Alternatively, you can simply shop by rooms: bedroom, living room, bathroom, dining room, kids' room, kitchen, office, patio & outdoor.

Overstock.com offers you apparels, shoes, pieces of jewellery, luxury watches, electronics, pet supplies and so many more. The catch about this site is that you can easily get products for your clients with expensive taste and that love to use quality, costly items. You don't get things for cheap here. The things you get here are quite expensive, and they are well worth it. Items procured here are meant to be sold to the elite group of people on your network who will appreciate it for its value and will not have issues paying the price you have set for the products.

You won't have to bother whether or not your clients are going to buy it. They have adorned costly items before and are now able to assess the quality of the merchandise you will be showing them.

4.   WWW.CARTERS.COM

Carters.com is exclusively for kids. Baby clothing, kids clothes, toddler clothes are the kinds of products you will find here.

If you love fashion, and you want to get nice and quality clothing for your kids, then this site is for you. Many may have heard of this site before, especially those that have shopped in the US before. They can attest that Carters.com is fast becoming a well-known name for babies' lovely clothes and fashion items.

It does not stop at clothes and fashion items. Whatever you can think of that makes for the total care and daily living of babies can be shopped on this site. Such include toys, napkins, bottoms, diapers, etc. Nonetheless, the site does not offer ingestible baby products such as food and baby groceries.

All the sites I have so far shown are US e-commerce sites. Therefore, for you to actually understand how to make good use of these sites for profiting in your mini importation business, you need to change the product prices from dollar to your local currency.

Before proceeding to show you some other handy sites for other niche, I will like to intimate you with one more fashion intensive e-commerce site. This time around, it is an Indian e-commerce site.

5.   WWW.MYNTRA.COM

As should be expected, the site is in English language, but the prices are set in Indian Rupee. Those in the US and other countries whose currencies value more than the Rupee stand a lot to gain from this site. They can leverage on this simple fact to make much profit.

Myntra.com is also a fashion intensive e-commerce site that caters to many categories of fashion products for men, women, and kids. Products from diverse popular brands are available for sale on this site too.

It is worthy of mention that the fashion trend nowadays has witnessed people taking their dressing cues from other cultures and backgrounds to dress. Even in my country, many people now wear the Indian Sari to important occasions. And it is not happening only here in Nigeria; it is obtainable in several other countries.

Colors
Embroidered Jacquard Fashion S...
Rs. 899 Rs. 2998 (70% OFF)

Kvsfab
Crepe & Silk Printed Saree
Rs. 1202 Rs. 3249 (63% OFF)

Ishin
Woven Design Mangalagiri Saree
Rs. 1079 Rs. 3599 (70% OFF)

Saree Mall
Printed Saree
Rs. 724 Rs. 2899 (75% OFF)

For an observant miniimportation businessman, this is an opportunity to market Indian fashion wears and accessories to those appreciative of the culture. People have, in like manner, profited and made hundreds of thousands of dollars from a fad. This though is not a fad; it does not seem to want to pass away anytime soon.

I have bought goods from this site. I have done my research; you do yours. What I deem inexpensive might not be cheap to you. You might also want to check out this site for yourself. On this site, you can find INVICTUS shirts, lovely and beautiful tops that you may want to explore. Some of these shirts are about $38.

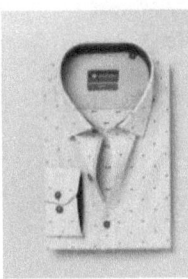

INVICTUS
Slim Fit Formal Shirt
Rs. 1379 Rs. 2299 (40% OFF)

INVICTUS
Men Checked Slim Fit Formal Sh...
Rs. 509 Rs. 1699 (70% OFF)

INVICTUS
Checked Slim Fit Formal Shirt
Rs. 1049 Rs. 2099 (50% OFF)

INVICTUS
Slim Fit Formal Shirt
Rs. 1259 Rs. 1799 (30% OFF)

These are shirts that sell at good prices after being imported.

Take a look at the nice shoes below. Trust me, as much as there are very cheap shoes on this site there are also those that are expensively priced. For example, you can get a pair of shoes worth about $134. Skechers is one of the brands that can be obtained here at a fair price. I personally do not go for the high-priced shoes; I go for the San Frissco shoes that cost about $17 – $22 to buy. If you are a guy and you know what I am talking about, when you see good shoes, you will know its value.

San Frissco
Men Derbys
Rs. 1118 Rs. 2795 (60% OFF)

San Frissco
Men Oxford Formal Shoes
Rs. 1318 Rs. 3295 (60% OFF)

San Frissco
Men Formal Shoes
Rs. 1318 Rs. 3295 (60% OFF)

San Frissco
Men Semiformal Slip-Ons
Rs. 1198 Rs. 2995 (60% OFF)

In the US, for example, you can put these on your online store, price it reasonably and make a good profit. Conversely, shoes are weighty and it might increase your landing costs. It is not advisable for starters in the business to deal in shoes first off.

Other e-commerce sites where you can get fashion items for both male, female and children include:

- www.10dollarmall.com
- www.payless.com
- www.apparelcandy.com
- www.ioffer.com
- www.wish.com
- www.6pm.com
- www.snapdeal.com
- www.flipkart.com
- www.jabong.com
- www.firstcry.com (exclusively for babies)

In considering why you need to opt-in for mini importation in the previous chapter, you were presented with the market data statistics for various categories of products. The phone market alone was valued at $532.2billion and the implication of this is that, if at the moment there are about 8 billion people on planet Earth, then for every 1 billion humans, $66.52billion is being expended on phones and its accessories. What a striking statistic!

Can you begin to imagine the kind of profit that is plausible in this market? It is a tenable market for achieving your financial goals in mini importation.

There is hardly any man in the 21st Century that does not make use of a phone in one way or the other. Everyday, billions of dollars exchange hands in the phone market; from the user to the call and Internet service providers; from the user to the phone repairer; from the phone repairer to the importer of phone spare accessories and so the cycle goes.

Simply put, there is always a need for phone and phone accessories. Imagine if everyone that has a phone at the moment decides to use an earpiece; imagine you were given the mandate to supply just a thousandth of this population in your city only; carefully analyze the kind of profit that will attend your way. Such is the potential of the phone and phone accessories niche.

The phones and gadgets niche comprising phones, phone accessories, laptop and laptop accessories, cameras, game accessories, etc. is one that you can decide to venture into in your mini importation business. The following sites offer you these items at relatively cheap prices from which you can maximize profits.

1.   WWW.CELLULARCOUNTRY.COM

They actually sell refurbished phones on this site. iPhones are sold here in addition to other brands of mobile phones you can think of. At a time when blackberry was being sold for about $165 – $195, it was for sale on this site for as little as $14.

Diverse brands of phones are available on cellularcountry.com and different categories of phones exist on this site also. You have to watch out carefully for the quality of what you want to purchase.

Based on their quality and newness, phones or in general, items on this site are classified as MINT, GOOD, EXCELLENT and FAIR.

MINT – refers to products that are like new.

GOOD – the products within this category have undergone normal wear and tear that comes with use.

EXCELLENT – refers to products that have a very little sign of use.

FAIR – represents products that are appreciably worn out.

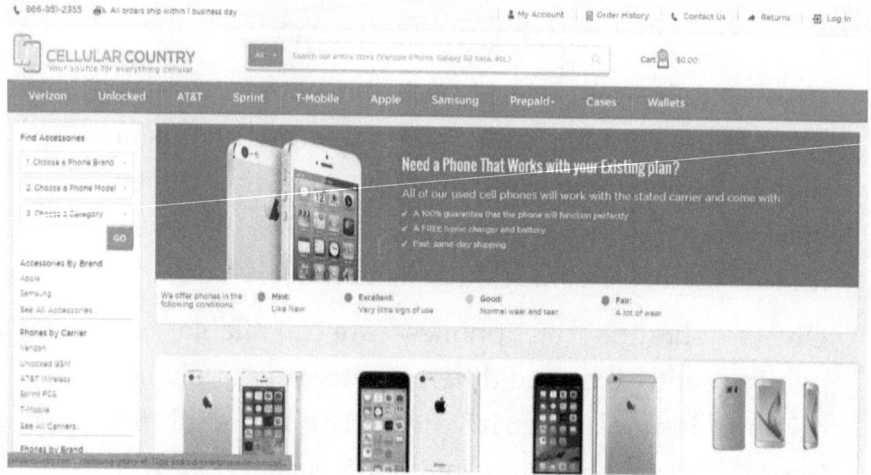

I advise you to go for products in the mint condition. The ones that are labelled mint signify that the phones have not actually been used. They only have a slight factory defect and have not been used; such defects may be that the mouthpiece doesn't function well etc.

For those in the excellent category; they have only a little defect that has now been fixed. The good ones too are like this; they were once damaged, but now are in good condition. You can visit this site for phone accessories and laptop accessories.

The first mentor I had for mini importation had an issue with his phone screen; it got damaged. He took it to computer village in Ikeja (Lagos, Nigeria) and asked for the price for fixing the phone screen. The repair guy actually charged him about $80 for purchasing the screen and $8.50 for the workmanship, and that was quite expensive. He then reasoned within himself; why will he spend that much on the repair of the phone to enrich the phone repair guy? Why can he not just visit cellularcountry.com and check if he could find the exact screen for his phone? Fortunately for him, he found it on cellularcountry.com. Both the purchase and shipping of the product cost only $2.75. In the process, he has saved for himself a little over $75. That would have been a colossal waste of money.

All he did was import it from cellularcountry.com, and gave it to the guy to fix the screen for the bargained $8.50. Therefore, if you know how to repair phones or laptops, this may be a niche you can focus on in the mini importation business. You can deal phone accessories. Many people than you can imagine have one issue or another with their phones. You can also delve into the purchase of earpieces, power banks, USB cords; you can actually go into them and make an extremely cool profit.

If you deal in phones and laptops, they carry a lot of weight. So, be ready to bear some shipping costs. If you are just beginning, then it is advisable for you to start with phone accessories instead of the phones itself. This will ensure the lightness of the goods you will be importing and save you shipping costs.

2.   WWW.DHGATE.COM

It is a Chinese e-commerce website in the English language so you do not have to bother about a language barrier. They charge in dollars even though it is a Chinese website; you then will have to convert the prices of goods to its equivalent in your country's currency.

The phones here are priced cheaply compared to what obtains on the various popular e-commerce sites you know. Just like what holds in cellularcountry.com, if you so desire, you could get refurbished phones here in different brands and models. Plus, you can find new phones here too. This is one way in which it differs from cellularcountry.com where only refurbished phones are being sold.

Here is a highlight of some brands of phones available on DHGate.com

Still in this niche are the phone and laptop accessories like earphones, chargers, USB cables, Bluetooth devices and many more. They are items people use on a daily basis, and many people have the need to replace theirs. This is a ready market; a profitable one at that.

These accessories can be obtained from this site at cheap prices and sold for the normal street price to make a huge profit. An example is as shown below:

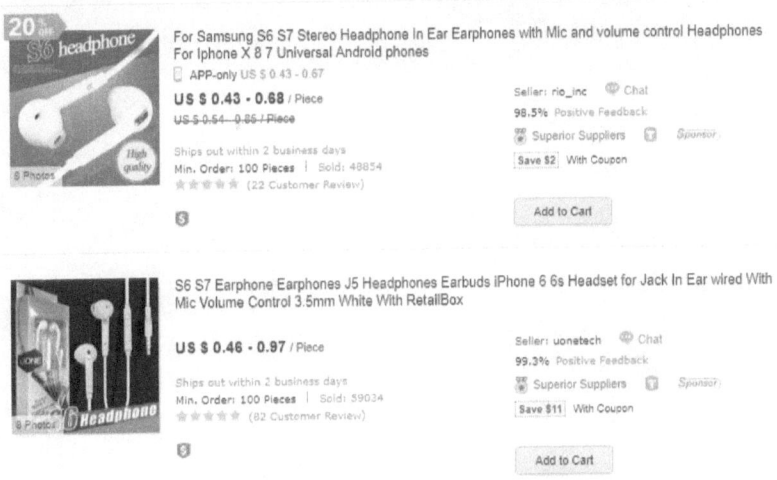

From the picture above, you will observe that DHGate.com has a minimum order quantity (MOQ) for items on their site. You stand to enjoy a price reduction as your order quantity increases.

The site is relatively easy to navigate and available to guide any new users on the site are seller ratings, rankings, and customer reviews. Make sure you go through these as a precautionary step to guide your purchase on the site.

Other e-commerce sites that will come in handy for anyone that wants to deal in gadgets; phones and phone accessories or laptop and laptop accessories include:

- www.newegg.com
- www.chinainvasion.com
- www.ebay.com
- www.ipmart.com
- www.dx.com
- www.bestbuy.com
- www.snapdeal.com
- www.infibeam.com
- www.lightinthebox.com
- www.ankaka.com

Another niche many other people have optimized for profiting is the car niche. Although a lot of caution is needed to venture into this category of mini importation, the potential for gain is also jaw-dropping. It makes the stress worthwhile. E-commerce sites that offer cars at such a low and importation-friendly prices are as follows:

1.   WWW.AUCTIONEXPORT.COM

Most of the fairly used cars in that abound around you were probably gotten from sites like this. Auction Export is a place where you can get cars that have been used but because they have been damaged in one way or another, they are now up for sales. On this site, you bid for cars. As you can see below, the current bid for this car is $25 and there remain 7 days for the bidding period for the car to end. The moment you find a car of your choice; you go ahead to make a bid for it.

How? You register with auctionexport.com and search for the cars that meet your requirement and bid. I always advise people not to on the day bidding starts; your bidding should start 2 – 3 days to the end of the bidding.

That way you will have monitored how people have been bidding.

Another unique thing about this site is that to register you must supply your detailed information upon sign up e.g. your account details; this is so that if the bid lands in your favour they will be sure you have the financial capacity to purchase the car. The amount in your account must be at least enough to get the car bided for. You will receive a call from them a day before the bidding ends when they are somewhat confident that the bidding might eventually be in your favour. The call is to confirm your readiness to take delivery of the car.

To aid you and provide a near accurate guide for you before you settle for any car, the site actually provides all necessary details you might need about the car to make the bidding/buying decision. So far, there has been a sizeable amount of reviews that attest to the authenticity and quality of the customer service that auctionexport.com offers. Just like I mentioned when I began talking about the site; most of the cars you find around you were purchased from this site. If you have been observant, you will have seen auctionexport.com stickers on most of the cars you have come across. With this kind of record, you can be sure that you are in good hands doing business with auctionexport.com.

Before you buy any of the cars, make sure to check everything about you're the car. It is advisable you don't get some category of cars here. For example, cars whose air bags have been let out, badly damaged because of water or accident; cars that have been involved in an accident before etc. It is my candid advice that you steer clear of these kinds of cars.

You have to carefully observe the details of the cars before you go ahead to purchase them. Another thing I want to say is that for these cars you don't actually ask them to fix it for you. They will want to know if you want the car fixed for you. Don't let them fix it for you because the cost of fixing alone can be higher than the cost price of a new car depending on the damage to the car.

For the Hyundai car displayed above, the following are the details provided on the site about the state of the car at the time of bidding.

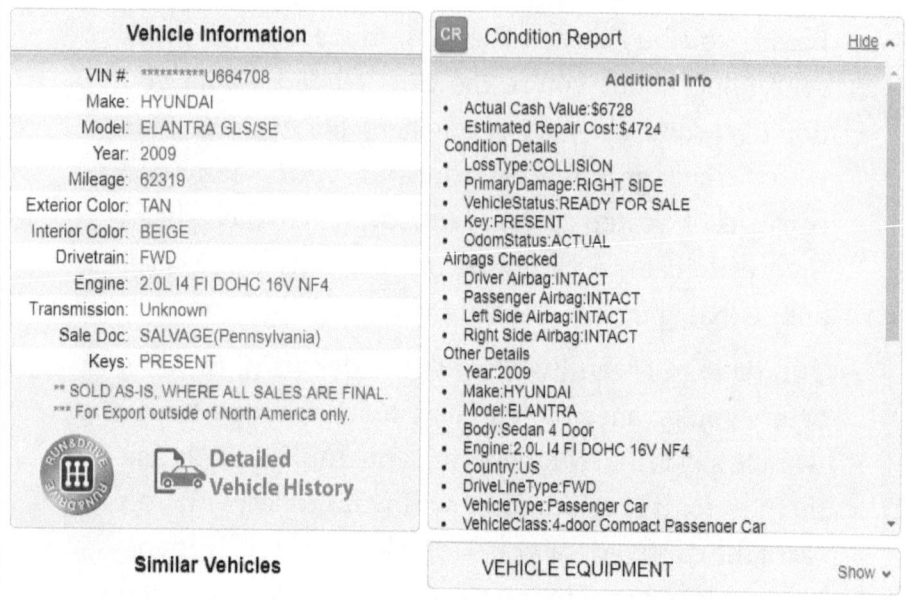

Vehicle Information

VIN #:	*********U664708
Make:	HYUNDAI
Model:	ELANTRA GLS/SE
Year:	2009
Mileage:	62319
Exterior Color:	TAN
Interior Color:	BEIGE
Drivetrain:	FWD
Engine:	2.0L I4 FI DOHC 16V NF4
Transmission:	Unknown
Sale Doc:	SALVAGE(Pennsylvania)
Keys:	PRESENT

** SOLD AS-IS, WHERE ALL SALES ARE FINAL.
*** For Export outside of North America only.

Detailed
Vehicle History

CR Condition Report   Hide ⌃

Additional Info
- Actual Cash Value:$6728
- Estimated Repair Cost:$4724
Condition Details
- LossType:COLLISION
- PrimaryDamage:RIGHT SIDE
- VehicleStatus:READY FOR SALE
- Key:PRESENT
- OdomStatus:ACTUAL
Airbags Checked
- Driver Airbag:INTACT
- Passenger Airbag:INTACT
- Left Side Airbag:INTACT
- Right Side Airbag:INTACT
Other Details
- Year:2009
- Make:HYUNDAI
- Model:ELANTRA
- Body:Sedan 4 Door
- Engine:2.0L I4 FI DOHC 16V NF4
- Country:US
- DriveLineType:FWD
- VehicleType:Passenger Car
- VehicleClass:4-door Compact Passenger Car

Similar Vehicles   **VEHICLE EQUIPMENT**   Show ⌄

In my country, what most people involved in car importation do is that they bring these cars into Nigeria and let their automobile mechanics fix it for them. I will advise you, if you don't know much about cars, get someone you know that is good with cars or your automobile mechanic to check out the site with you; going through all the car specifications shown on the site.

When the customer care representative at auctionexport.com discovers that the bid for a particular car will be in your favour, they will reach out to you via a voice call to congratulate you and instruct you on what to do for you to take delivery of your car. You are to make sure you have sufficient money in your auctionexport.com account to pay for the car you have bided for. If you do not, the next person whose bid comes after yours will be contacted to take delivery of the car.

A number of other sites that can be of similar business advantage to anyone choosing this niche in the business include:

- www.falconsgt.com
- www.autopartswarehouse.com
- www.diecastdiscount24.com

Remember, I had said earlier that one of the major demands of this business is continuous research and learning. All the e-commerce sites listed and briefly discussed above are products of my thirst for knowledge about this business and tireless research. The e-commerce sites that you can get products from to build a highly profitable and scalable mini importation business are nevertheless, not exhaustible.

You may have wondered why I have taken the time to showcase these sites. One of the reasons is to make you see the price disparity that exists on the popular e-commerce sites that people and probably you shop from compared to the ones I have just unveiled for the same level of quality products.

The following real-life stories attest to this:

- A few months ago, there was a need to urgently replace one of the laptops in our company. I told the man assigned to carry out the purchase that, but for the urgency of the moment, I could have helped out in buying the choice laptop at a relatively cheap price. After much ado, he proceeded to get the laptop.

  On getting to the market, he met the laptop at a whopping sum of $972. He was amazed and was taken aback. Even though he is renown for his good negotiation skills, he was unable to get the item at a lesser price. While he was out to get the laptop, out of curiosity, I visited the different e-commerce sites I patronize for my mini importation business; I found the exact same laptop at a ridiculous price.

  When he returned to the office; I was the first to call him and inquire about the price at which he procured the laptop. I shook my head upon hearing the price – $972 – "that is way too much," I blurted out. I bade him to follow me to my office where I showed him the exact same laptop at $480. He could barely hide his bewilderment. It was written all over his face.

Can you imagine? He got the laptop at more than double the price for which the manufacturer had sold it. Even at that, the seller was all boastful, saying he was 'just' giving it at a price of $972, a fair pricing on his part.

Such is the way these folks make money off people. They exploit the ignorance of people for an outrageous profit.

- This second event I want to share is more like the first. It even has a humorous twist to it. I had posted pictures on Facebook and ran an advert for my upcoming seminar. That was just one of the many seminars I held weekly at our office location here in Nigeria.

On the set day of the seminar, one of the staff working with me to put the seminar together was putting on the exact shirt I had used to run the advert. Out of curiosity, I asked the amount at which he bought the nice shirt. He replied "$40." I smiled wryly.

I told him to pay attention to my presentation during the training because I am sure something on one of my slides will catch his eye.

He got to know from my presentation that the same shirt he thought he purchased at a fairly reasonable price of $14 actually goes for just $3 on one of the e-commerce sites I taught on. He was aghast. Before he saw the shirt at a lower price he was of the opinion that $14 was a fair price to pay for the shirt.

Should I decide to detail many of such encounters that I have had in my pieces of training and contacts with people, then I might have just written another book. The common denominator in all those scenarios is that people who thought they had negotiated well and obtained products at a fair price become surprised when they discover that the products are available at a way cheaper price than they could imagine.

Although I have revealed a couple of sites to you here, you might be so impressed that all the categories of goods you found on those sites because of the quality of pictures used to represent the products are appealing to you. In spite of that, you need to exercise prudence.

In the light of this, let me send a note of caution to you. Stress is inherent in a myriad of choices. Having many e-commerce sites to patronize to begin and thrive in this business model can be overwhelming. You are laden with the burden of choice: choice of niche, choice of sites to import from; payment options and many other decisions you might have to make to successfully have your goods in your home country. Meticulously consider this benign truth; there are people that are earning 5 – figures per month just by carrying out a market research cautiously and locating one viral product to meet the needs of a desperate market. Indeed, there is no cap to your earning potential in this business if only you pay the price to be careful in getting necessary information about selecting a niche and meeting the need of a hungry market.

Recall that I earlier emphasized on the need to have a focus in this business. Being a generalist does not sustain long-term business growth. If you should settle for diverse niches at any one time, you will only discover that you are always busy without proofs of productivity – results.

ORDERING FROM THE US E-COMMERCE SITES
MyUS.com

It may seem that I have laden you with the responsibility of getting delivery of your products from the United States. While this may be a non-task for those living in the US, it however is a challenge that needs to be laid to rest for many that are not in the US nor living in border countries to the US like Canada and Mexico.

The internet is to the rescue. Moreover, many have taken up this as a vocation – to help with getting orders delivered in good time. Therefore, for the mini importers, non–resident in the US or any of the two border countries listed above; www.myus.com is the go-to site to make shipping to your country stress-free and economical.

All MyUS members receive our world-class customer service and express door-to-door delivery options. Cancel or change at any time!

	SINGLE PACKAGE	FREE TRIAL PREMIUM	+ MAIL
I WANT TO SHIP:	One Package from One Store	Packages from Multiple Stores	Multiple Packages & US Mail
MyUS Shipping Discount ?	✓	✓	✓
Premium Shipping Discount ?	20%	20%	20%
US Tax-Free Shopping ?	✓	✓	✓
Free Package Consolidation ?	—	✓	✓
Free Package Repacking ?	—	✓	✓
Free Package Storage ?	—	30 Days	30 Days
Monthly Fee	No Membership Fees	FREE	$25
Compare all features	SIGN UP	START FREE TRIAL	SIGN UP
		$7/month after 30-day free trial	

Cancel or change your membership at any time.

To start with, you need to sign up on the site and follow through with the registration process. In doing so, make the information you are supplying on the site is accurate.

After signing up for the site you will be expected to select a membership package that you desire. It brings you the different packages available on the site which you can choose from and kick-start with them. Click on the 'sign up no membership' package pending the time you have fully evaluated the plans and are ready to make the choice that you are sure is befitting for your business use. Let your choice of a plan be based on the frequency with which you intend to order from the US e-commerce sites.

Next is the avenue where you will be required to supply your billing information. This aspect of your getting started on the site is crucial as it is an avenue for your account to be verified on the site. When you follow through with their lead, $1 will be deducted from your account to make for your account verification; to check if whether or not it is active.

While filling in your billing information, check the box 'billing address is the same as shipping address'.

How to Ship With MyUS.com

When you are shipping with this site, you are expected to supply any US e-commerce site this address (given to you by MyUS.com) as your delivery address. When putting in your card details on any e-commerce site make sure it is the exact same one you used for your MyUS.com registration to make for easy verification of your account on the purchasing site before you can start out using them.

This is how it works: You are to shop on any US e-commerce site like normal adding as many products as you desire to cart. When you are about to check out the items in your cart; you are expected to simply supply the unique address given to you by MyUS.com to the site. They then will ship your goods to MyUS and MyUS will get your goods to you safely.

You may want to ask, why not get the e-commerce site to deliver the goods directly by themselves? The answer is short and simple; it will cost more. Your goal for using MyUS is to make for investment cost optimization.

ShopToMyDoor

Those residing in the US have no need for this site as they do not ship to the US.

The site is easy to navigate and makes for easy use. It also requires that you sign up on the site before you begin using their services.

If you can determine the dimensions of your product then there is provision for you to get the shipping cost that will accrue to you. All you need to do is fill the form below:

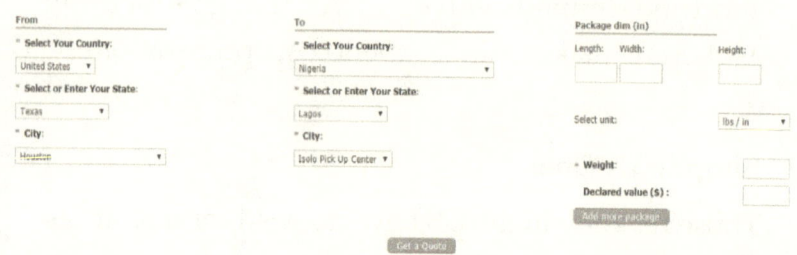

However, if you could not determine the dimension of the goods, there is no need to worry, there is also provision for that:

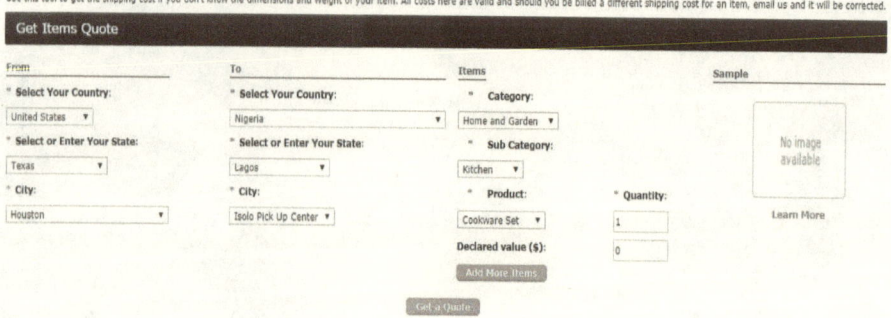

Just like MyUS, when you sign up here, you will be assigned a unique address which you will use for shopping on US e-commerce sites.

Your assigned address allows you to shop in the US (UK and China for some customers) using the following simple method.

- Go to any store of your choice, shop and pay with your visa, mastercard or Paypal.
- Send all purchases to your assigned address. I.e Your assigned address is your shipping address.
- Shop as much as you want. You have 21 days free storage to shop in as many stores as you want, and we combine all in your warehouse.
- We alert you via email and SMS once any item is received for you.

For clarity, after signing up:

- Go to any US e-commerce store of your choice, shop and pay via any means of payment most convenient for you

- Send all purchases to your assigned address, i.e. the address given to you by shoptomydoor.com

- You have 21 days free storage to shop in as many stores as you want and shoptomydoor.com will combine all in your warehouse with them

- You will be alerted by email and SMS once any of your items is received for you.

Within the 21 days or a few days after, when you are ready to take delivery of your goods from your warehouse with shoptomydoor.com, simply log in to your warehouse on the site and select the shipment for shipping.

Shoptomydoor.com will require outright payment from you for shipping; your goods will thereafter be shipped after which you will get it in your hands in a few days.

In the next chapter, I will be showing to you one more site. I went for a desperate search for this site because I was convinced at heart that there must exist a site where I can get goods directly from the manufacturers. I knew this will exponentially increase my profitability and give my mini importation business a new outlook; it will eventually be the catch for me. Voila! I found it! Ever since then this one site has become one-million-sites-in-one to me. And that is what it really is.

Let us delve deeper into the dynamics of this site as I unveil it in the next chapter.

CHAPTER 3

MY ULTIMATE E-COMMERCE SITE

Ignorance is one of the reasons why many are poor today, and I mean that not only in financial terms but in diverse facets of their lives. What you do not know cannot work for you; it cannot add to you neither can you maximize its full potential. In fact, the status quo of many today is a direct consequence of their ignorance. Worse yet is the illusion of knowledge that has left many in a vegetative state where they have become blinded to the seemingly obvious truths that abound around them. They will not acquiesce that there are pedestals they have not yet accessed. However, facts do not cease to exist simply because they are ignored. Benjamin Franklin said that "Being ignorant is not so much shame, as being unwilling to learn."

Life is all about responsibility; it is, however, somewhat pathetic that many come to this assertion too late in their lifetime. According to Jim Rohn, "You cannot change the circumstances, the seasons, or the wind, but you can change yourself. That is something you have charge of." You have the charge to turn your life around in all ramifications.

The major obstacle we have to overcome in our quest for success and breakthrough in life is ignorance. Every man you know, thriving and recording huge success in any area of endeavour have access to information that has eluded others like him in the same profession or a field of endeavour. This is not to say that the requisite information is inaccessible to anyone; not so many people are ready to give what it takes to access such information. Nothing of value comes free.

This above saying holds true irrespective of what you do. Whether you are a doctor, a lawyer, a fashion designer, a handyman, a bank teller or even a farm worker; it does not matter at all. What is significant for your upward scaling of new heights in your business and vocation is access to pertinent knowledge. You must, nevertheless, understand that execution will beat knowledge any day.

This is because knowledge is power, potential power. Potential and results are two extremes. We all must strive to make sure that to the knowledge we garner action is added. What happens if we don't do something? Either it never happens, or someone else gets a shot at it instead of us. If something is for sale, and we know it is worth more than it is selling for, and we do nothing about it; someone else will get to it eventually, right?

At this juncture, I want to congratulate you for taking the bold step to start your mini importation business. I hope by now you have seen how costly ignorance is. You have seen how sellers are making stupendous money off the ignorance of many shoppers. You have decided to have a change of mindset about importation and attune your ears to this guide; in that, your emancipation from your status quo has just begun.

Being a timely business; for profit maximization in mini importation, the businessman must always be on the lookout for information and hurriedly take consistent action; searching for new sites that products can be procured relatively cheap from. I cannot overemphasize the need for continuous search and research for anyone intending to go into this business. A lot of learning is what it takes to make a headway. Learning about new emerging markets; hot-selling products in each of the different seasons within a year; locations where some products can make stupendous turnover and more. The list is endless. Timely access to information in this business will amount to profit multiplication for the mini importer.

Without the need for rocket science; there are two sites anyone venturing into the importation business must be aware of. And yes, they are the two sites on your mind at this point as you are reading this book:

1. www.alibaba.com

2. www.aliexpress.com

ALIBABA.COM

As of 2014, Alibaba.com, the primary company of the Alibaba Group, was the world's largest business-to-business trading platform for small businesses. Alibaba.com, English Language portal of Alibaba Group handles sales between importers and exporters from more than 240 countries and regions of the world.

Alibaba is the largest Chinese e-commerce company. In fact, the company is really a collection of smaller companies cobbled together into a holding company. For example, one of Alibaba's most important constituents is Taobao; a consumer e-retailer often thought of as the eBay of China. As for comparisons to existing companies, Alibaba.com is most often compared to Amazon.com. Although major differences exist, both companies have advanced business lines in retailing, wholesaling, group buying, cloud computing and payment systems.

Earlier, I mentioned that your profit was inherent in where you procure the products you have decided to deal. If you are able to get quality products from a site like www.alibaba.com, imagine the massive profit that will result from your sales.

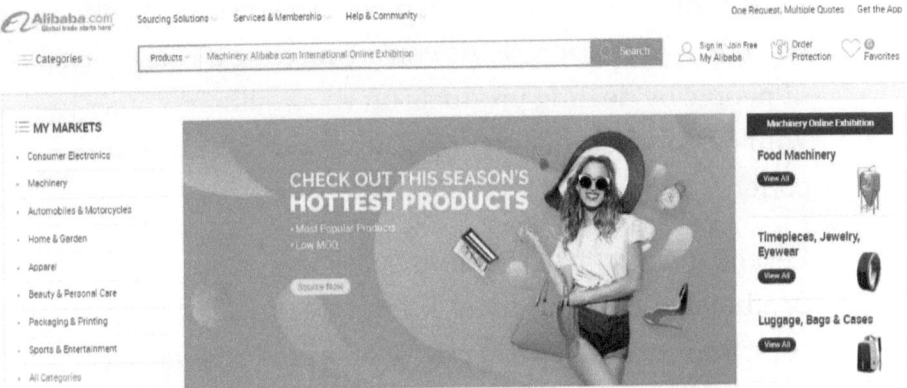

Alibaba.com has established an unbeatable big name on the global market of wholesale trade and almost all merchants know well about it. This is one site millions of people have used all over the world to their financial advantage; there is no reason why you should be left out.

According to Jack Ma, the recently retired Chairman of the Alibaba Group, "If a company can serve two billion consumers, that is one-third of the total population of the world. If a company can create 100 million jobs, that is probably bigger than most governments can do. If a company can support 10 million profitable businesses on its platform, this is called an economy."

Mind you, these are not mere speculations. They are educative statistics. Imagine you are laden with the responsibility to serve a fraction of the whole world with the amazing products you can procure on this site. You will not need to struggle. As you are meeting the needs of people by dealing products on www.alibaba.com, your customers, will, in turn make deposits into your coffers.

Let me quickly take you to the site to explore some products. While at that, I implore you to keep comparing the quality and prices of the products we find to the ones we checked out on Amazon. Pay attention to the prices, especially. It is for good reasons that Alibaba.com is regarded as the Amazon.com of China. Let us quickly observe the pricing of some select products in different categories available on www.alibaba.com.

Cool Racer back mandala
peacock feather print maxi

US $7.99-9.99 / Piece
10 Pieces (Min. Order)

Indigo Tie Dye Maxi Length
Sleeveless Rayon Crepe

US $7.1-8.4 / Piece
1 Piece (Min. Order)

Long sleeve floral rayon print
casual dress guangzhou women

US $7.2-8.8 / Pieces
100 Pieces (Min. Order)

BestDance Ladies 1920s 20s
Party Dress Flapper Costume

US $8.99-13.99 / Piece
1 Piece (Min. Order)

Italian shoes and bags to
matching New Design african

US $35-43 / Set
1 Set (Min. Order)

2017 Hot selling high heel
shoes and bags/top quality

US $50-60 / Set
1 Set (Min. Order)

BCH33 Queency New Coming
African Women High Heels

US $40-50 / Set
1 Set (Min. Order)

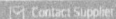

Women's Sexy Point Toe High
Heels Patent Leather Pumps

US $31-39 / Pair

MYLOVE E1488 New Women
Long Chain Bling Ball Drop
Price: US $2.69 / Pair
MOQ: 24
Recently orders: 1

High Quality Stainless Steel
Buddhist Om Mani Padme
Price: US $3.88 / Piece
MOQ: 20
Recently orders: 0

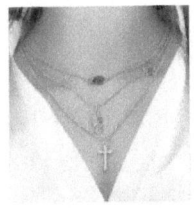

New products 2016 Fashion
Jewelry , 18k plated cross
Price: US $1.1 / Piece
MOQ: 20
Recently orders: 1

High quality 24k saudi gold
jewelry in unique designs
Price: US $3.98 / Set
MOQ: 12
Recently orders: 0

92

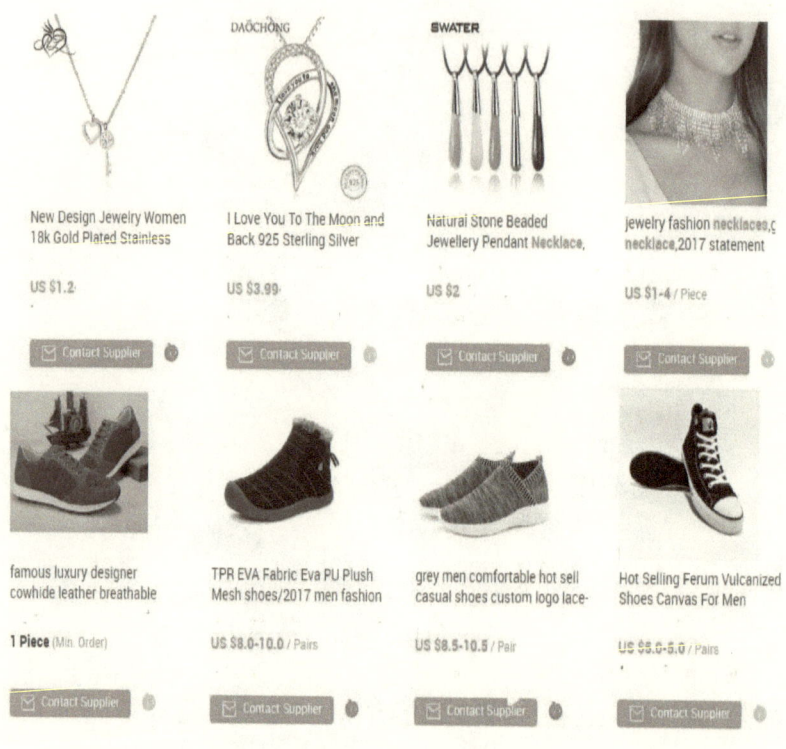

New Design Jewelry Women 18k Gold Plated Stainless

US $1.2

I Love You To The Moon and Back 925 Sterling Silver

US $3.99

Natural Stone Beaded Jewellery Pendant Necklace,

US $2

jewelry fashion necklace,c necklace,2017 statement

US $1-4 / Piece

Contact Supplier

famous luxury designer cowhide leather breathable

1 Piece (Min. Order)

TPR EVA Fabric Eva PU Plush Mesh shoes/2017 men fashion

US $8.0-10.0 / Pairs

grey men comfortable hot sell casual shoes custom logo lace-

US $8.5-10.5 / Pair

Hot Selling Ferum Vulcanized Shoes Canvas For Men

US $5.0-5.0 / Pairs

Contact Supplier

The above products are only infinitesimal samples of the products obtainable on the site at the prices stipulated. Check out the site for yourself. You are sure to come across various products you have bought, used or even gifted out before.

Customer reviews abound in the millions on the site. There are several thousand reviews on products on the site that will guide you in making a purchase on the site.

You are afforded the opportunity to get a sincere evaluation of products and customer service of the seller of the product from customers like you.

Additionally, Alibaba.com has a link on the top right hand of the home page where you can easily access the products of sellers in the Top Trade Assurance Suppliers category. This is like an authenticating seal from Alibab.com herself. You can be sure you are dealing with genuine suppliers or bulk resellers directly.

Really, there are diverse millions of products available on this site cutting across different categories such as:

- Machinery / Mechanical Parts / Tools / Hardware
- Consumer Electronics / Home Appliances / Security
- Auto / Transportation
- Apparel / Textiles / Timepieces / Accessories
- Home & Garden / Construction / Lights / Furniture
- Beauty & Personal Care / Health
- Packaging & Printing / Service Equipment
- Electrical Equipment / Components / Telecom
- Sports / Gifts / Toys
- Minerals / Chemicals / Plastics / Energy

- Bags / Shoes & Accessories
- Food & Beverage / Agriculture

These major categories are further divided into many other subcategories for ease of site navigation. You could also search for products of your choice using the search bar provided on top of the page. This way, whenever you are not sure of the category your choice products belong, you won't have to go on a wild search.

Moreover, when your search is done and you have a wide array of products to choose from, on the left-hand side on the site are parameters that you can tweak to your taste such that the products displayed on your screen will be those that meet your set specifications.

You will observe that products on this site seem to be even quite cheaper than the ones available on the US e-commerce sites that we earlier explored. The reason is not farfetched. We have discussed it earlier in previous chapters. China is now the largest manufacturing country in the world and they possess a magnanimous workforce. The cost of production of items in their country is relatively low. Now consider the impact these results into given that they are utilizing advanced technology to supplement their production processes.

Just like the many other sites we have explored, to shop on Alibaba.com you will have to sign up and set up an account with them.

Free shipping exists for some products on the site but that might mean many days of waiting which might not work for you. There are shipping options provided by shipping companies like DHL, FedEx, EMS, UPS etc. to aid you in the shipping of your goods to your country. Some of them charge exorbitantly. Be careful to read their terms and be okay with what they are offering before selecting the shipping agents you want to use for your products.

ALIEXPRESS.COM

Launched in 2010, Aliexpress.com has since grown to become the leading destination for small-scale importers

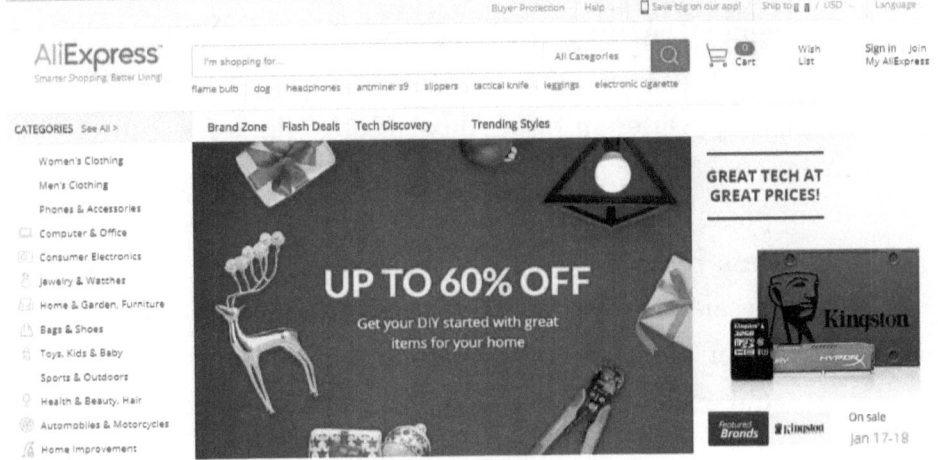

looking forward to buying goods from China at wholesale price. In actuality, it comprises small businesses in China and other countries of the world offering a diverse myriad of products to international online buyers. Simply put. It is an online retail store.

It is also often regarded as the 'Chinese Amazon'. AliExpress.com is a tool used by the Alibaba Group to expand its reach outside of Asia and challenge online giants like Amazon and eBay. You can find virtually anything for sale on the site. As an individual that wants to go into the mini importation business, you must understand that Aliexpress.com acts only as an e-commerce platform hence it does not sell products directly to customers.

In general, **AliExpress** is a global retail marketplace offering quality products at factory prices in small quantity. Different from Alibaba.com, AliExpress.com does not charge any fees on registered members (either suppliers or buyers) and inspects the whole transaction process between the two transacting parties. It's a wholesale platform targeting small and medium-sized suppliers and buyers. There are minimum order quantities as low as 1 item accepted and express delivery is available, in some cases, fast and free shipping is offered. In addition, a vast array of item categories can be found on AliExpress.com — it truly is a one-stop-shop for small, wholesale orders.

Bear in mind, AliExpress.com is a transaction-based retail website which allows **smaller buyers to buy small quantities** of goods at wholesale prices; herein lies the major difference between Alibaba.com and AliExpress.com

In a similar fashion as Alibaba.com, there are billions of goods available for sale on AliExpress.com. You will be taken aback by the kinds of products you will find here. It is almost as though you are buying from Alibaba except for the major difference I have quipped above and of course, the price disparity of products available on both sites.

At a click, you can navigate the site to check out such product categories as shown below:

- Women's Clothing
- Men's Clothing
- Phones & Accessories
- Computer & Office
- Consumer Electronics

- Jewellery & Watches
- Home & Garden, Furniture
- Bags & Shoes
- Toys, Kids & Baby
- Sports & Outdoors
- Health & Beauty, Hair
- Automobiles & Motorcycles
- Home Improvement

Obviously, selecting any of these categories leads you to other several categories you can choose from to narrow down your product search.

The value you obtain from the products shopped here is massive. This is added to the fact that AliExpress delivers goods shopped on their site worldwide. So, it does not matter which country of the world you are in; you can be sure of getting the goods you purchased on this site as at the stipulated time of delivery.

You have the option to pay with any of the world's most popular and secure payment options on AliExpress. Add this to the 24/7 round-the-clock assistance provided for you to have a smooth shopping experience; all you need to shop with confidence on this site has been perfectly kept in place.

Should you ask around, these two sites are majorly the sites that various startups and beginners in the importation business use to source for products upon which they build their businesses.

I know you might have wondered why I had not made mention of AliExpress or Alibaba in the previous chapter. You might even have wondered if the ultimate e-commerce site for my mini importation business is one of these two popular sites listed above. Well, you will have been wrong if that was your guess.

In a moment, before unveiling this site, I think it will be worthwhile to briefly intimate you with my first experience in the mini importation business; about the first order I placed for some products and how I have hitherto thrived.

Like many of you, when I got wind of this business model, I was ecstatic and resolute with the zeal of an iron to make the most of the opportunity. I could foresee the mammoth earning potential it has and how it will be a source of sizeable additional income for me. With my arsenal of knowledge consequent upon the pieces of training and research I had done then, I ordered my first batch of products.

I patiently waited for the goods for what seems like forever and could barely hold my peace when I was called that the goods have arrived. After taking delivery of my products, upon unpacking, I was somewhat discouraged. The products were nice and really good. In fact, they were the exact products whose pictures I have seen on the e-commerce site where I made the order. The descriptions of the products were as accurate as anyone would expect and I was holding what I had only seen as a picture online a few days ago live in my hand. What put me off was that most of them had 'Made in China' labels on them.

I could not understand why and how the goods I had ordered from a United States e-commerce site should have 'Made in China' labels instead of the 'Made in US' labels I was expecting. This particularly was the cause for my slight discouragement.

Another reason why I was discouraged is that, in my country – Nigeria, many are of the opinion that Chinese products are of inferior quality. The country, China, has become synonymous with low – quality materials; hence, I was afraid I might not be able to sell the goods as I had **SMART**ly acquired. However, that goods are made in China does not mean they are of inferior quality; my years of experience in the mini importation business have proven this to me repeatedly.

Nothing will appease me till I know why I got the 'Made in China' goods from a US e-commerce website. So, not so long after the episode, in the course of my search, I discovered that China has infiltrated the markets in virtually all the nations of the world. Many people now know this; There is hardly any country you will go without coming across 'Made in China' products. In fact, several companies from different parts of the world and from every continent go to China to have their manufacturing done for them to minimize the cost of production that could have accrued.

This is a list of companies who either own factories or have contracted factories producing their products in China. Some of the companies produce 100% of their products there, and others only produce parts or certain ingredients for their products. The list below is only a good few of the actual corporate list:

- Apple Computer
- Cisco Systems
- Black & Decker
- AT & T

- General Electric
- General Motors
- Toyota
- Dell Computer
- Caterpillar Inc.
- Ford Motors
- Victoria's Secret
- Google
- LG Electronics
- Samsung
- Gucci
- Nike
- Qualcomm
- Walmart
- Nestle
- Nixon
- Philips Electronics
- Sony
- Pfizer Inc.
- UPS
- Yahoo

I could go on and on. The above is a non-exhaustive list of American Companies who manufacture in China. I believe you might even have thought before now that some of these companies are Chinese companies.

What more proof would you require to affirm that goods from China are not low-grade products? In 2010, China displaced the United States of America as the largest manufacturing nation in the world. Three years later, in 2013, China widened the gap between them and the US in the quota of manufacturing done. As proof and attestation to this, the United Nations acclaimed China as having the largest manufacturing economy in the world which keeps growing rapidly annually. If the 25 companies listed above and many others find China a perfect place for the manufacture of their products, then China is gold. The earlier you clear your doubts about China, the earlier you started making cool cash from her.

For me, the unveiling of this truth created in me a new thirst. After months of being in the importation business, I hungered to know how to buy directly from manufacturers instead of wholesalers on e-commerce sites. I went from one training to another until I finally found the key. Now I can start mini importation and make 3 times my investment capital. This e-commerce site is not known to many. A lot of people still shop on ALIEXPRESS and ALIBABA without knowing that they are dealing with the **wholesaler,** not the **manufacturer.** The money you will use to buy a particular product on either site will procure 4 or more items on **my ultimate e-commerce site**.

MY ULTIMATE E-COMMERCE SITE

This site, which I now refer to as **my ultimate e-commerce site**, is a jackpot site. Except for cars, there is virtually no product, in any category imaginable that cannot be found on the site. What makes this so phenomenal is that products obtained from the site are directly obtained from the manufacturer. The site brings you to close proximity to the manufacturer, and in that, your profit margin is increased because you have eliminated the additional costs that could have been placed on the products by a wholesaler.

With this site, your mini importation business is at an all-time high advantage. You are provided with an array of diverse goods in several categories some of which includes fashion, sports, baby products, crafts, pets and gardening needs, phone gadgets, electronics, packaging materials, textile leather, etc. to mention a few. The wonderful thing about this site is that, because you are getting the goods from the stables of the manufacturer, you get the products at a ridiculously cheap price. The prices are so ridiculous to the point of being unbelievable.

It is then you will realize how expensive some products' prices are in your home country. You will also begin to see the great potential this business has.

Without any more ado, my ultimate e-commerce site is:

www.1688.com

This is the site that will avail you an uncapped earning potential. It is the site that will turbo-charge your mini importation business even if you are already in the business before now. It will serve as a good starting pedestal for anyone who is yet contemplating starting a mini importation business.

Even though Aliexpress, Alibaba and 1688 are all Chinese sites, yet it is somewhat unbelievable to see the extent of disparity in products pricing on Aliexpress and Alibaba compared to 1688. This is another proof of direct dealing with product manufacturers.

Have you bought products from Alibaba.com or AliExpress.com before now? Some have bought before and are yet purchasing. The truth is, if you are still buying things from Alibaba.com or AliExpress.com you are actually wasting money.

To make this clearer to you let me distinctly show you the difference between the three e-commerce sites – they are all owned by the Alibaba Group.

- Alibaba.com is the world's largest online business-to-business trading platform for small businesses. This portal handles sales between importers and exporters from more than 240 countries and regions.
- AliExpress.com is a transaction-based retail website offered by AliExpress.com, which allows smaller buyers to buy small quantities of goods at wholesale prices.
- The Chinese portal 1688.com was developed for domestic business-to-business trade in China. In

2013, 1688.com launched a direct channel that was responsible for $30 million in daily transaction value.

Inherent in the pristine purpose behind the creation of 1688.com is the reason for the extreme cheapness of products found on this site.

The platform was created for the citizens of Chinese. Therefore, as expected, prices of in–country goods are way cheaper than the ones meant to be sold to business owners in other countries.

This also is what amounts to the profiting of anyone using this platform to source for goods to sell as a mini importer. You will be getting goods here as though you were resident in China. Your profiting is sure irrespective of how your country's currency is valued against Chinese Yuan.

To prove this to be true, examine the following product selection ideas:

There are products that are really inexpensive and very profitable; the wristband is one of such products. Wristbands are stupendously cheap and the good news is that on this site, they are customizable for the buyer by the manufacturer. This category of goods is best suited for those that want to venture into the mini – importation business without sizeable capital at hand. This is because the goods are of lightweight and the cost of importation due to weight becomes drastically reduced.

Let us look closely at the profit potential of the wristband business:

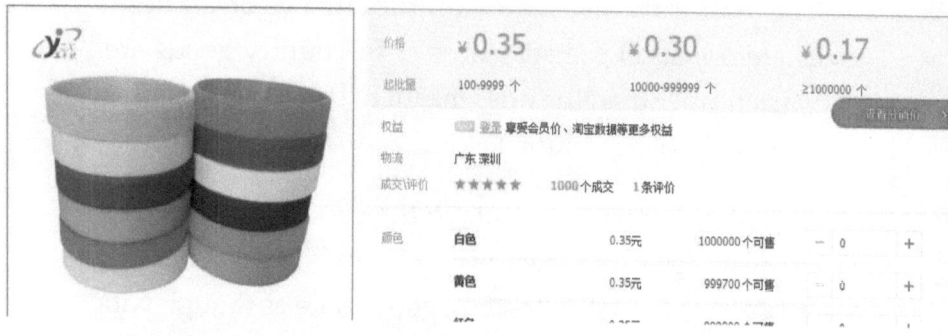

From the website, one wristband goes for at most $0.05. This is just 5 cents.

Ordering for 1000 units will, therefore, amount to a total cost price of $50.

I hope you now see that I was not being unrealistic when I mentioned that you could start your mini importation business with as little capital as $55.

As said earlier, there is already an investment cost minimization resulting from how light the product is compared to computer accessories, laptops, and even lace fabric. Lace materials carry a lot of weight hence it is not advisable for starters with low capital in the business to deal in it.

The wristband would not be demanding of much capital for clearing when it eventually lands in your country. A thousand units of the wristband will barely weigh 2kg. Let us set the weight of the whole wristbands though at a maximum 2kg.

If we assume the shipping costs to be $ 10 (which is actually too much to assume); this totals the cost of investment to be $60. I don't know about your country but here in Nigeria, the minimum a wristband of the sort displayed above is sold for is $0.60 (60 cents).

Therefore, on just 1,000 wristbands, assuming you are giving it out at the street price of $0.60, you will sell your whole merchandise for $600 leaving you with a profit of $540. What's more! The market for wristbands is not going down anytime soon. There is barely anywhere you will go in your country without spotting people using a one branded wristband or another.

Many manufacturers on 1688 offer customizing services to buyers. They can help you customize the wristbands to bear any logo of your choice and your customers will only be amazed at the quality of products they will be getting. Remember, all these will be done without leaving the need for you to leave the comfort of your home; you are just leveraging the power of the internet.

Let us take a look at another example of a product you can deal to make a ridiculous and stupendous profit. If you think the wristband avails an awesome earning opportunity, then I am sure this will blow you away.

The product is a diaper. Yeah. You saw that right. The next product whose profit potential we will be considering is a diaper. Businesses have profit making as one of their major objectives else bankruptcy is inevitable. The expensiveness of what you are dealing is not what matters but the profit it brings into your coffers. You do not need to trade items like shoes, phones, gadgets, fashion and fashion accessories before you start making a gigantic profit in mini importation.

You could earn a monthly 4 – figure income trading socks and other forms of hosiery only. I want you to observe my choice of products so far. I have been careful to only go for products with a hot ready market and that are lightweight. This is to ensure that the landing cost of the goods will not be expensive, thereby prompting the spending of more cash.

Quickly, let us analyze the profit potential available in the diapers niche:

You might be wondering, how much can one make from selling diapers? Let me show you:

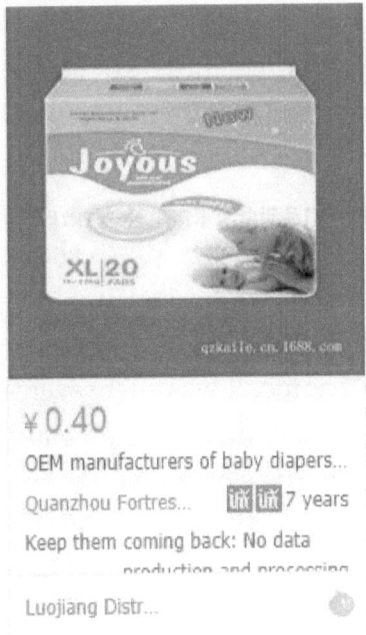

¥0.40

OEM manufacturers of baby diapers...

Quanzhou Fortres...   [logo][logo] 7 years

Keep them coming back: No data

production and processing

Luojiang Distr...

One pack of the diaper, from the manufacturer on this site, costs only $0.60 (I mean 60 Cents, not $6). Can you imagine that?

Now, on other online stores and in most marketplaces, this particular brand of diapers goes for $5.00

Wow! What a jaw-dropping profit potential this product category avails.

The least amount of packs you can cart from the manufacturer is 500 units. The cost of investing in this product will, therefore, amount to $300.

Now, assuming the goods are cleared with the weight in perspective for $40; when you sell the whole 500 units of diapers you will have a turnover of $2,500.

Your profit, therefore, is $2,160. This is mind-blowing profit.

One of the things that people underestimate or do not understand while venturing into the mini importation business is that one does not just go diving in; there are lots of findings. The products I have used as examples above are products of one of the many findings I have made. Some people get stranded because they did little or no research; they just go buying seemingly cheap products. I have once done that too. It was after several trainings that I discovered how wonderful and pivotal it is to be mentored in the ways of the business.

NAVIGATING 1688.COM
Overcoming the Language Barrier

Unlike what holds on the other popular Chinese sites we have earlier explored that are in the English language; 1688.com is entirely in Chinese. This therefore gives rise to the first challenge you might encounter with the site. Personally, it took me a little while to get over this. It is actually a simple thing to do being made easier by the extensions and plug-ins that come with the browser you are using.

To get over this, it is easier if you are using a Google Chrome browser. You will need to download the Google Translate extension. Follow the steps below to achieve this:

- Go to 'More tools' by clicking on the three vertical dots on the top right corner of the browser window

- Click on 'Extensions'

- Scroll to the bottom of the page and click on 'Get more extensions'

- Search and install 'Google translate'

Having done this, whenever you load the 1688.com site, you will be able to automatically translate the site from Chinese to the English language and navigate the site with ease.

This picture above shows what the site looks like after installing the Google Translate extension and before translation.

If you are using Mozilla Firefox browser, all you need to do is to download the S3 translator plug-in. To do this:

- Go to the 'Tools' menu on your browser toolbar and click on 'Options'

- Click 'General'

- On the next page, click on 'Manage add-ons'

- If you do not already have the plug-in, go to 'Get more extension'

- Type the search query 'S3 translator'

- Install the plug-in and you are good to go

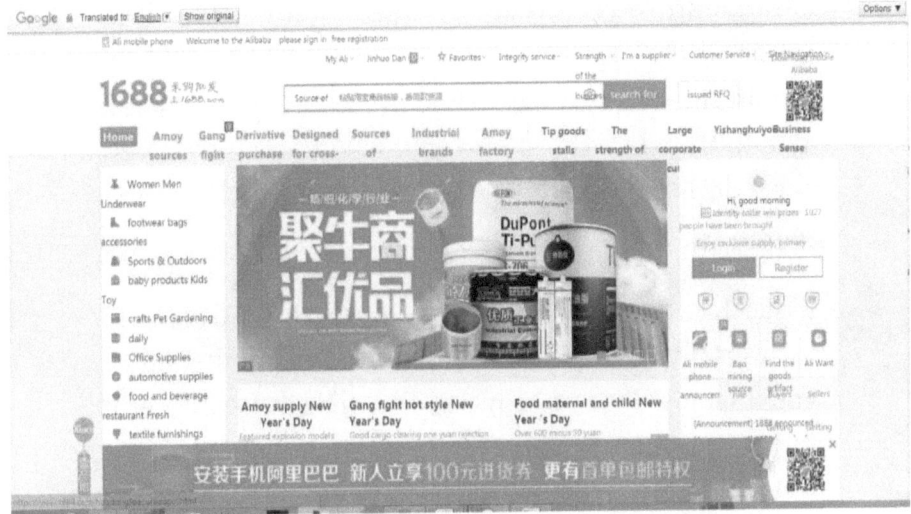

Before proceeding to show you how to search for goods on this site, kindly note that you are not expected to sign up on this site. It is in this wise different from Alibaba.com and Aliexpress.com. It is exclusively meant for residents of China. There is a way around ordering choice goods from this site; I will go into the details of that in the next chapter. For now, bear in mind that you are not to sign up or register on this site.

Searching for Goods

Peradventure you were not able to get your desired goods via the site navigation tabs on the left hand side of the site; this is no cause for alarm. Since you have been able to translate the site to English language, all you need do is to type the product of your choice in the search bar and submit your search query.

If this does not work out as perfectly as you had wanted, then simply load translate.google.com on another tab of your Google Chrome browser. Translate the search term to its equivalent in the Chinese language; copy the resulting translation and paste in the search box on the 1688 site. This should give you a better search results that you had obtained in your previous trial.

How to Get 'Made in Europe' and other brands of products.

Open the site and search for the type of fashion wear you desire.

Go to the style settings and click on the country whose products you want to get.

As an example, I will search for 'beautiful gowns'. Thereafter, I will try to use the method described above to get the ones 'Made in Europe'.

While browsing through the site, I am sure you are amazed at the prices of the products you are coming across; you are also taken aback by the pictures you are seeing. This is good and for the most part, real. However, you must be cautious while surfing this site; you do not just go for any beautiful product you see. There are fraudulent individuals on the site posing as manufacturers of products, but really are only wholesalers trying to make money off unsuspecting shoppers. The good news is that there are ways of fishing them out and avoiding their traps.

In fact, some authentic manufacturers may not have bright and high-quality images of their products on the site. This does not in any way connote the inferiority of their product.

The following are the foolproof ways of identifying genuine manufacturers and products:

1. Going through the comments/reviews on a product.

To start with, the more comments a product has, the more the reliability of the manufacturer/supplier. This is proof that many people have purchased the products and have one or two helpful things to say about it.

It is left to you to carefully go through these comments and take the comments of previous consumers about the product under advisement.

Each reviewer of any product also has the option to rate the product in stars. Most of them assign stars that are reflective of their view of the product. Use this as a guide also.

2.   The number of people who have bought the product.

It has often been said that the voice of the people is the voice of God. It is rare for many people, by many; I mean thousands of people to patronize a particular manufacturer for a specific product if the product or the manufacturer is fraud.

For instance, the seller of the manufacturer of the shoes above has been able to make 11,317 sales; 4331 customers have also taken their time to review the product after taking delivery. This is good data to work with. All you need to do is read carefully through the comments to know what to expect or watch out for as you decide to order for these shoes.

These two tools, combined together can help you wade your way through the numerous manufacturers/suppliers on the site.

There you have it; **my ultimate e-commerce site** explored and explained. This one site has made a memorable, drastic and undeniable positive change in my business. Since the discovery, I have made gigantic profits that are almost unbelievable for most of my small investment capital. It has been a most rewarding experience transacting business using 1688.com.

Using this site, I have mentored consistent monthly 5 – figure earners in mini importation using 1688.com. Many of them were at an all-time low financially; mini importation was their bailout.

I have good news for you. With a continuous commitment to learning and seeking out sites that are similar in operations to **my ultimate e-commerce site– 1688.com,** I found two other sites, namely:

- www.taobao.com

In May 2003, Alibaba Group founded Taobao as a consumer e-commerce platform. As of 2013 was China's largest consumer-to-consumer online shopping platform. The main difference between AliExpress and Taobao is that it is aimed primarily at international buyers; mainly in the USA, Russia, Brazil or Spain.

- www.Tmall.com

In April 2008, Taobao established Taobao Mall (www.Tmall.com), a retail website, to complement its consumer–to–consumer marketplace.

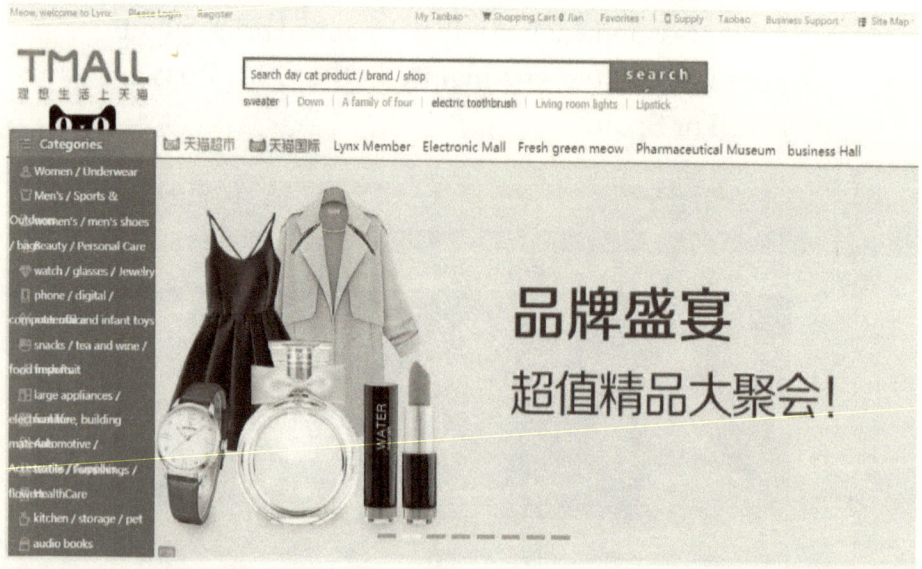

It became a separate business in June 2011 and as of October 2013, it was the eighth most visited website in China.

Both sites, Alibaba's consumer-to-consumer portal, Taobao.com, and business-to-consumer portal Tmall.com, each feature nearly a billion products and both are among the 20 most visited websites globally. Can you imagine that? Almost a billion products to profit from on both sites.

These sites have a close resemblance to 1688.com in that they are owned by Alibaba.com and I have chosen to unveil them to you for your careful consideration and profiting. You have no inhibition in using them to your advantage. You could cross-examine prices of products that fit into your selected niche and go for the ones that will avail you maximum profit.

SECURED PAYMENT – ALIPAY

If you attempt to shop on any of the e-commerce sites owned by the Alibaba Group, you will often come across the Alipay option and might have wondered how it works. It is actually an escrow that helps to build your trust and confidence in the safety of making payment on the site you are shopping on.

You may not know this, but in 2013, Alipay overtook PayPal as the world's largest mobile payment platform. At the moment, Alipay has a facial recognition payment service. This should buttress your confidence in shopping on any of Alibaba.com, AliExpress.com, 1688.com, Taobao.com, and Tmall.com.

For consumer protection, Alipay provides an escrow service, in which buyers can verify whether they are happy with goods they have bought before releasing money to the seller. You will not need to bother about whether or not the products that will be delivered to you are genuine, top – quality or not. The moment you get it and are not satisfied with what you received, you refuse the product and inform Alipay about the order rejection. Consequently, Alipay will not release the money for the products to the supplier.

This goes a long way to solve the trust issues many have with shopping and paying online. More so when there is no option for Cash on Delivery (COD) on the site they are shopping on. An escrow such as Alipay is appropriate in order for the parties involved, that is both the seller and especially the customers not to be cheated and thus helps protect them. The Escrow keeps the money until the customer receives the products satisfactorily before the money is released to the seller.

To use Alipay, you will have to register on the portal and set up your financial account with them using your card: Visa, MasterCard, Discover or others. Alipay accepts quite a number of cards.

At this juncture, I presume you have developed a passion for the business and can barely wait to get started with ordering your products. Well, not so fast. There are yet some things I will be opening your eyes to see for you to successfully start out your mini importation business. Therefore, consider the following important things in the next chapter before you place your order.

CHAPTER 4

STARTING OUT WITH YOUR ORDERS

Hitherto in this sojourn that I am taking you through, I have been able to help you understand the need for: selecting a niche; setting and having SMART business goals/plans; devotion to continuous research and I have unveiled a most phenomenal site to you that can literally positively turn around the profitability of your mini importation business.

However, potential and manifestations are different. Our potentials only give an insight as to the kind of result we can command. It is our tactful investment in the potential that takes us to our desired end where our proofs speak louder than our voices.

There are yet many things you need to learn about shopping with 1688.com in starting and building your mini importation business. These are the little things that make the difference between the successful mini importer and the one that seems to be failing. It is, therefore, my candid advice that you pay particular attention to the following items. They will go a long way to give you an enjoyable ride in the world of mini importation.

SELECT A NICHE

This aspect of the business cannot be overemphasized. Remember what I said about focus; it will go a drastic length in helping you build momentum, reduce stress to a barest minimum level for you, increase your engagements with your current clients and while at that, will attract more customers to you. Good news travels fast; your excellence in product and service delivery will be obvious and the people you have been privileged to sell to will help you put a word out to others who then will become itching to patronize you.

As I have said severally, there are multiples of categories of products/goods to deal in while venturing into mini importation. Some popular ones are as highlighted below; let it also serve as a memory jogger for you. You could write down as many product ideas that come to your heart as you go through the list:

Electronics

- Phones, phone accessories (earpieces, selfie stand, etc.), tablets, phone cases, protective packs, phone screens, screen guards, power bank, hair clippers etc.

- Laptops, laptop chargers, mouse, Bluetooth, mp3 players, memory cards, USB cords, flash drives, cameras, RAM, solar chargers, headphones etc.
- Reading lamps, extension socket, chandelier etc.

Beauty Products/Accessories

- Jewellery, necklace, earrings, bracelets, bangles, rings, beads etc.
- Human hairs, Brazillian hairs, synthetic-blended hair, feather hair, wigs etc.
- Ladies make – up kits, blushers, eyelashes, eye shadows, lipstick, mascara, nail polish, artificial nails etc.
- Powders, creams, perfumes, body sprays, electronic body massagers etc.

Apparel & Accessories

- Men's clothes, Women's clothes, Kids' clothes etc.
- Underwear, shirt, jeans, blouses, skirts, scarves, shoes, sandals, belts, wallets, bags, handbags, purses, caps, **flip-flops** etc.

Office Equipment

- Files, rind binders, bulldog clip, folders, glue stick, tape dispenser, rubber stamp, hole punch, highlighter, marker, staple remover, correction fluid, sticky notes, card index, furniture etc.

Other Products

- Packaging materials, toothbrushes, combs, sponges, nail clippers, spoon, kitchen utensils, nutcrackers, grater, corkscrew, bottle opener, tin opener, mugs, wines, beverages, detergents, textiles, mechanical fittings, lights, chandeliers, pet supplies etc.

The list of products is not exhaustive. Do not be surprised that I included flip-flops under the Apparel & Accessories category as one of the products you can deal. You will be surprised at how much you could make from it. The story below illustrates this.

In 2017, a man in Nigeria was arrested by the Economic and Financial Crimes Commission of Nigeria. This was prompted because he had bought a house worth $1.4m when only a few months before he had barely $1000 in his account. After many investigations into his account, he was released when they found that he had legitimately earned his money by importing flip-flops from China to sell in Nigeria. (In Nigeria, there is virtually no home that does not own at least one flip-flop)

By now, you should learn that your product niche might not need to sound so magnificent for it to turn into profits for you. Hitherto, we have seen how much you stand to gain from the importation of flip-flops, diapers or wristbands. And those are just three of numerous light weighing products that have a high turnover rate. Other examples include chokers, eyelashes, handkerchiefs, socks, underwear, jewellery etc.

Did you know that even after selecting a niche, you could go further and opt for a sub-niche? Yes, you can. This is more specific and narrows down the products you will be ordering a great deal. For example, if you say your selected niche is Beauty Products, there are several thousands of products in this category. On the other hand, if you go further to focus on human hair under beauty products, then you have drastically reduced the variety of products you will be dealing. In addition, selected you can still narrow it down this niche to wigs only. Even in the wigs sub-niche, you could at the same time decide to go for purely braided wigs. I hope by now you know how this works.

For the many people I have been privileged to mentor in this business, one thing I particularly emphasize for them as beginners in the business is that they should as much as possible, go for lightweight products. This will ensure that an inherent cost minimization is in place without cutting down on their profit potential. Going for lightweight products drastically reduces the landing cost of the goods and the cost of importation in total.

This permits you to price your merchandise slightly lower than what obtains in the marketplace to make for speed of sales, customer acquisition and gives you an edge over competitors.

Already I have given several examples of lightweight products to deal to emphasize the importance of starting your mini importation business with light-weight products. This point is worth the iteration I am giving to it. It is one of the reasons many mini importers get frustrated from the outset of their mini importation business.

More on The Fashion Niche

For those intending to go into the fashion niche, there is yet something you need to pay attention to so you can sell with ease and not have difficulty meeting customers' needs.

To start with, you must have selected a niche you are sure you can start your business with. Then you have to bother about the sizes of the products you will be ordering – shoes for men, women and kids, rings, underwear.

Before you go ahead with your order for products in this category, find out the commonest sizes of fashion products and accessories consumers in your locality/country are using. This should be a guidepost for your order placement and the quantity you will be ordering. You might have to mix the sizes of the products you will be getting.

Next, since the 1688.com site is in Chinese and is a Chinese site too, we know that all sizes seen on the site are Chinese measures. You, therefore, must be able to find the equivalent of these Chinese measures in your country's measure. This is not to say that every country has a unique means of measurement. Many countries adopt the measure of some other countries around them. For example, there are many countries around the world whose means of measurement are exactly the same as that of the US.

I have tried to give you a chart to guide you and help you convert these Chinese measurements of shoe, apparel and jewellery size into the equivalent of the scale used by other popular countries.

Men's Shoes Size Conversion Chart

Korea (mm)	240	245	250	255	260	265	270	275	280	285
Japan (cm)	24	24.5	25	25.5	26	26.5	27	27.5	28	28.5
US	6	6.5	7	7.5	8	8.5	9	9.5	10	10.5
Europe	38	38.5	39	40	40.5	41	42	42.5	43	44
UK / Australia	5	5.5	6	6.5	7	7.5	8	8.5	9	9.5
China / Hong Kong / Taiwan	38	39	40	41	42	43	44	45	46	47

Men's Clothing Size Conversion Chart

International	XS		S		M		L		XL
Korea	90		95		100		105		110
Japan	36	37	38	39	40	41	42	43	44
Japan	S		M		L		LL,XL		
US			36		38		40		42
UK			36		38		40		42
Australia			36		38		40		
France			46		48		50		52
Italy			46		48		50		52
China	160/80A	165/80A		170/84A	175/88A		180/92A	185/96A	

Women's Shoes Size Conversion Chart									
Korea (mm)	220	225	230	235	240	245	250	255	260	265
Japan (cm)	22.5	23	23	23.5	24	24.5	25	25.5	25.5	26
US	5	5.5	6	6.5	7	8	8.5	9	9.5	10
Europe	35	36	36.5	37	38	38.5	39	40	40.5	41
UK	3	3.5	4	4.5	5	5.5	6	6.5	7	7.5
Australia	4.5	5	5.5	6	6.5	7	7.5	8	8.5	9
China / Hong Kong / Taiwan	34	35	36	37	38	39	40	41	42	43

Measurement References							
Chest (cm)	72-79	79-86	86-92	92-98	98-104	104-109	109-115
Waist (cm)	63-70	70-76	76-81	81-86	86-91	91-96	96-101
Height (cm)	155-165	155-165	165-175	165-175	175-185	175-185	175-185
Chest (inch)	28-31	32-34	35-36	37-39	40-41	42-43	44-45
Waist (inch)	24-27.5	28-30	31-32	33-34	35-36	37-38	39-40
Height (inch)	61-65	61-65	65-69	65-69	69-73	69-73	69-73

Female Clothing Size Conversion Chart								
International	XS	S		M		L		XL	
Korean	44	55	66	77	88				
Japan	5	7	9	11	13	15	17	19	21
US	0-2	4	6	8	10	12	14	16	18
UK / Australia	4-6	8	10	12	14	16	18	20	22
France	32-34	36	38	40	42	44	46	48	50
Italy	36-38	40	42	44	46	48	50	52	54
China	160-165	165-170		167-172		168-173		170-176	
	84-86	88-90		92-96		98-102		106-110	

Measurement References								
Bust (cm)	78-80	81-84	84-89	90-94	95-99	100-105	106-112	113-118	119-125
Bust (inch)	30-33		34-37		38-44			45-49	
Waist (cm)	61-63	64-68	68-71	72-76	77-81	82-88	89-96	97-100	101-108
Waist (inch)	24	25-30			31-34		35-37	38-42	
Hip (cm)	83-86	87-90	91-95	96-100	101-104	105-110	111-117	118-125	126-131
Hip (inch)	33-35		36-39			40-46		47-52	

For plus – sized women, the following charts will come n handy

For Suits & Jackets (cm)									
Size	15	17	19	21	23	26	30	34	38
Bust (Standard)	92	96	100	104	108	114	120	126	132
Bust (Plus-size)	97	101	105	109	113	119	125	131	137
Waist (Plus-size)	76	80	84	88	92	98	106	114	122
Hip (Plus-size)	101	103	105	107	109	114	118	122	126

For Skirts & Pants (cm) - Extra Wide Sizes												
Size	73	76	80	84	88	92	96	98	100	104	106	108
Waist	73	76	80	84	88	92	96	98	100	104	106	108
Hip (Standard)	97	99	101	103	105	107	109	112	111	113	116	115
EW (Extra Wide)	99	101	103	105	107	109	111	114	113	115	118	117
2W (Double Wide)	101	103	105	107	109	111	113	116	115	117	120	119
3W (Triple Wide)	104	106	108	110	112	114	116	119	118	120	123	122

For Tops, Bottoms & Shorts (cm)								
Size	L	2L	3L	4L	5L	6L	7L	8L
Bust	86-94	93-101	100-108	107-115	114-122	121-129	128-136	135-143
Waist	69-77	77-85	85-93	93-101	101-109	109-117	117-125	125-133
Hip	92-100	97-105	102-110	107-115	112-120	117-125	122-130	127-135

For kids' apparel:

Babies Apparel Size Conversion Chart		
Age (months)	Body Length (In)	Body Length (cm)
Newborn	20.5	52
0 - 3	23	59
3 - 6	26	66
6 - 9	29	73
9 - 12	31.5	80
12 - 18	33.5	85
18 - 24	35.5	90

Girls Age	Kids Size	Height (in)	Height (cm)	Boys Age
			Kids Apparel Size Conversion Chart	
2	80	31-33	78-83	2
2	85	33-35	83-88	2
2	90	35-37	88-93	2
2	95	37-39	93-98	2
3-4	100	39-41	98-103	2-3
3-4	105	41-43	103-108	2-3
4-5	110	43-45	108-113	3-4
4-5	115	45-47	113-118	3-4
5-6	120	47-49	118-125	5-6
6-7	130	49-53	125-135	7-8
8-9	140	53-57	135-145	9-10
10-11	150	57-61	145-155	11-12

For kids' shoes:

Age	cm	EU (Europe)	UK	USA	Japan
			Kids Shoe Size Convertion Chart		
	12.5	21	4.5	5.5	12.5
	13	22	5	6	13
	14	23	6	7	14
	14.5	24	7	8	14.5
2-5	15	25	8	9	15
	16	26	8.5	9.5	16
	16.5	27	9	10	16.5
	17	28	10	11	17
	17.5	29	11	12	17.5
	18.5	30	12	13	18.5
	19	31	12.5	13.5	19
6-10	19.5	32	13	1	19.5
	20.5	33	1	2	20.5
	21.5	34	2	3	21.5
	22	35	2.5	3.5	22

For ring sizes:

Ring Size Conversion Chart					
Ring diameter (mm)	Inner circumference (mm)	Japan	HK	US	UK / Australia
13	40.8	1	---	1	C
13 ½	41.9	2	3	2	D
13 ⅔	42.9	3	5	2.5	E
14	44	4	6	3	F
14 ⅓	45	5	7.5	3.5	G
14 ⅔	46.1	6	8.25	3.4-4	G-H
15	47.1	7	9	4-4.5	H-I
15 ⅓	48.2	8	10	4.5-5	I-J
15 ⅔	49.2	9	11	5	J
16	50.3	10	11.5	5.5	K
16 ½	51.3	11	12	6	L
16 ⅔	52.4	12	13	6.5	L-M

16 ⅔	52.4	12	13	6.5	L-M
17	53.4	13	14.5	6.5-7	M-N
17 ⅓	54.5	14	16	7-7.5	N-O
17 ⅔	55.5	15	17	7.5-8	O-P
18	56.6	16	18	8	P
18 ⅓	57.6	17	19	8.5	Q
18 ⅔	58.6	18	20.5	9	R
19	59.7	19	22	9.5	S
19 ⅓	60.7	20	23	10	T
19 ⅔	61.8	21	23.5	10-10.5	T-U
20	62.8	22	24	10.5	U
20 ⅓	63.9	23	25	11	V
20 ⅔	64.9	24	26	11.5	W
20 ⅔	64.9	24	26	11.5	W
21	66	25	27.75	12	X
21 ⅓	67	26	29	12.5	Y
21 ⅔	68	27	30	13	Z

PRICE COMPARISON

After selecting a profitable niche upon which you have decided to build your business, reach a conclusion on the products you want to buy and make sure to compare the prices of the products on 1688.com and other platforms that I have shown such as Alibaba.com, AliExpress.com, Taobao.com, and Tmall.com.

This should inform you and give you a sense of value for the product you want to buy.

Furthermore, you might want to compare the price of the product as given by different suppliers on 1688.com. Do not just go ahead to procure goods on the first search page. You might discover that the product is being given away for a lesser price than the previous prices you might have seen on 1688.com.

Nonetheless, do not be distracted by your lookout for lower pricing that you forget the guideposts for confirming the authenticity of a manufacturer and his product: number of transactions recorded by the manufacturer and the number of reviews on the product.

NEGOTIATING WITH THE CHINESE MANUFACTURERS

One of the reasons why it is good to broker with a supplier is that it helps you to bring down your product price to a lower amount. For example, the products we have analyzed their profit potential can have their prices further reduced by the manufacturer if we are able to connect with the manufacturer and with good negotiation skills, get the prices beat down.

For you to negotiate with them there are two ways:

1.   The first way is through a social app called QQ. You can download it by visiting www.imqq.com. An activation message will be sent to you within 24 hours. Get the QQ number of the Chinese supplier and then you can start chatting with him. However, not every manufacturer you are buying from have their QQ number displayed along with the product on 1688. In this case, what you need to do is download another app.

For the Chinese, the QQ app is like their own WhatsApp or BBM. For them, it is a live app that runs on their phones 24/7. Using this app, your message in English will automatically be translated to Chinese for them and for you it will automatically translate the message you receive in Chinese to English.

2.   You can download the Alibaba trade manager. Go to www.trademanager.alibaba.com It is, however, time-consuming. I mean this in the sense that whatsoever it is that you are saying in English must first be translated to Chinese before sending it to the supplier and upon the receipt of the supplier's message; you will have to translate the received message to English for your understanding.

In case your seller does not have his QQ number displayed along with the product, connect with him on trade manager. As you download and install it; chat him up and request for his QQ number. He will forward you the QQ number.

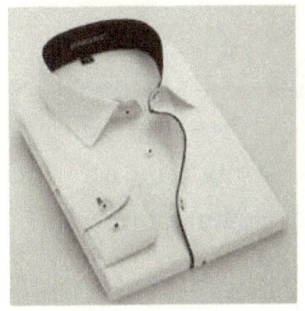

¥ 33.00   30 Tian turnover o...
Men's shirts long-slee...   advertising
Wang Yiwu efforts...   three years
Keep them coming back...
15 00c   of production and processing
Zhejiang Yiwu

Now let us use the shirt below as an example:

The blue button is where to connect to the Chinese supplier on 1688 using QQ. Their QQ number is there.

In order to make it easier for you when negotiating, you can arrange your products in Excel format. It helps your supplier to see how much you are negotiating. That will help your negotiation go down well.

There you have it; that is how you negotiate with the Chinese supplier.'

One other reason for negotiation:

Besides price comparison, there is one other reason why you should connect with the manufacturer. This is to order for a test quantity of the product you desire to start dealing on a very large scale. This is like a foretaste of what you will be trading in consequent times. This helps you to personally handle the product, use it and evaluate it live before you start dealing the product on a large scale.

This step is very important because there is a need for you to go beyond just seeing pictures and reading reviews to decide on a product you might be ordering subsequently in several hundred or even thousands.

GETTING RELIABLE FREIGHT FORWARDERS / PAYMENT

Freight forwarders are third party agents, like middlemen that can help you with bringing your goods into your county and reliably handle your payment to the manufacturer.

They are available in every nation of the world. There are so many of them in China, United States, Dubai, United Kingdom, Nigeria and many more nations.

Of course, they also have their office(s) situated in China. They will help you transport your products from China to your home country. All you need to do is send them the links to the products you are buying; they will get the links and the products you want to buy. On your behalf, they will pay the supplier and bring your goods to your country.

When your products arrive in your home country, you pay them their statutory charge for helping you get your goods into the country. This charge is always preset so you can have an idea of what you will pay as soon as your goods arrive. They charge per 1kg hence how much you pay will be based on how weighty your goods are. This has been the cause of my unending emphasis on ordering lightweight goods.

I have seen cases where the price some importers pay for clearing their goods is at times more than or slightly equal to the amount they spent to buy their products from the manufacturer.

One interesting thing about these freight agents is that they make the whole work less stressful. You can find them in your country. They are available in every nation of the world. If you have difficulty in locating them simply seek help online and put a word out to your friends and those in your network so they can help you with relevant information about them.

For those in Nigeria, the following are freight agents in Nigeria, their contact and operation details:

- **Nonikings Express(Express Shipping)**

  5, Oshitelu Street, Computer Village, Ikeja, Nigeria.

  China Contact: +8615813302441

  +8613128691487

They also offer for 2 – 3 days shipping depending on what you desire. For surety, you can visit their office in Nigeria.

- **Jeff Kizito Cargo**

  Personnel Unit, MMA Ikeja

  China: +8613434215425, +8615218866075

  Nigeria: 08162508815, 08033521291

- Base1:

  China: +8615018485486

  Nigeria: 08187878000, 08034865256

It is not compulsory you use these agents I am suggesting. The point is they are the freight agents I have used before and for some, I still am using them. I am giving their details for those that might be interested. Whatever transaction you do is solely with them. I am not accountable for any transactions taking place between you and the freight agents. You have to do your research very well about whichever freight agents you intend to use.

For those outside Nigeria:

If you are not resident in Nigeria, you can use FreeShoppingChina.com. Anywhere you are, they will service your importation needs. They are only a bit more expensive than other freight service companies that may be operational in your country. They also give a list of other sites that you can buy from; nevertheless, they are all Chinese sites. Personally, I work extensively with 1688.com.

For you to start using the site, you will need to sign up and register an account with them by filling in relevant registration details.

- Sign in and click on the shopping cart icon. Then go to 'members center'.

- Proceed to add order now.

To place a shipment order for any product you want to buy on 1688.com, all you need to do is copy the link to the product (from the address bar of your browser) and paste it on this site. As you paste the link, it will automatically upload the product you are buying on FreeShoppingChina.com.

We Are Purchase Agent Helping You Buy/Purchase From China

Communication	Payment	Surface Inspection	Packaging	Shipping
We help you communicate with Taobao/1688 sellers.	We make payments to Taobao/1688 sellers for you.	We stop inferior/incorrect items for you.	We consolidate your items with safe packaging.	We offer different discounted international shipping methods.

We Support Purchase On:

1688.com(Alibaba.cn Wholesale)   TaoBao.com(Retail & Wholesale)   Tmall.com(Retail)

`https://detail.1688.com/offer/554579562491.html?spm=b26110380.sw1688.mof001.154.K0R` Add An Order Now

Try Adding A Item Page URL Here and FSC Will Purchase It For You!
(Example: http://item.taobao.com/item.htm?spm=a230r.1.0.0.0IRZ9q&id=39062207687)

Upon the submission of the link, you will be redirected to another page. A product link is peculiar to that product so there is no chance of mistaking one product for another.

The new page you are redirected to require that you fill a form for quantity and other specifications that are relevant for a detailed order placement.

Once you submit the form, you again will be redirected to another page. At this juncture, you have to transfer money to their account. To do this, you must have funded your FreeShoppingChina.com account. In fact, you should do this before you actually start purchasing your goods. It takes like 3 – 5 days for money sent to your FreeShoppingChina.com account to reflect. Once you have recharged your FreeShoppingChina.com account, you are free to pay for this site.

These are their account details:

>ACCOUNT NAME: WANG LANG

>ACCOUNT NUMBER: 6212998604748422

>SWISS CODE: CMBCHKHH

>ADDRESS: 21 Bank of America, Tower 12 Harcourt Road, Central, Hong Kong

You can then send a mail to service@freeshoppingchina.com with your necessary FreeShoppingChina.com account details – your username, product links and other information you perceive might be relevant.

Also, make sure whatsoever you are buying does not cost higher than the money in your account. Therefore, go about this patiently, calculatedly and carefully.

HOW TO PAY

This is also a very crucial part of shipping your products. Many keep asking, "How do I pay?" How to pay is very critical. If you want to pay you can use a PayPal account. Simply connect the PayPal email of the supplier, log in to your account and send the money.

Over time, the subject of how to pay has been one of the major concerns of online shoppers. In fact, this was what prompted the Alibaba Group to create Alipay. Alipay has since been used on all the e-commerce platforms owned by the company and many other platforms that receive payment online.

PayPal, however, is the option most accessible by all the parties involved in the importation – the manufacturer and you. It is also one of the trusted global platforms for financial transactions. There is hardly any country where PayPal is not being used. Hence, this is the option you will be using to pay for your goods.

With the help of the freight forwarders you are using, paying directly into the manufacturer's account for your goods have become easy. The email address used by the manufacturer for his or her PayPal account can be retrieved for you while you go ahead to make the payment. Your freight forwarder will confirm the payment and you can then go right on expecting your goods.

If a client is saying he doesn't want to use PayPal for the payment, know that there is something fishy about the client and do not buy from him.

SHIPPING PERIODS AND ORDER TRACKING

With your experience shopping online you know already that these two terms are norms of online shopping. The goods you have in your cart at checkout are assigned an order number and you will be told when to expect your goods based on availability and your location.

The same goes for the purchase you are making on 1688.com (and all the others I have showcased hitherto – Alibaba.com, AliExpress.com, Taobao.com, TMall.com). The goods you are buying have a preset shipping time depending on their nature and your country. More importantly, your freight forwarders are the indispensable in this process.

The timing for the arrival of your goods in your country is largely dependent on the freight forwarders you employed to do your shipping for you. This is because they are the ones that will do the procurement of the goods for you; they have already built and fostered a good working relationship with the manufacturers. They facilitate the relative quick arrival of your goods.

Normally, if you were to ship directly from these sites, you perhaps might be tempted to go for free shipping. Goods that are shipped free are often slated to arrive in 5 – 7 weeks depending on your country of residence. On the other hand, if you were to select some of the popular shipping companies to do the shipping on your behalf, then you will accrue more costs. Companies like DHL, FedEx, UPS, Red Star Express and the likes charge exorbitant amounts for their shipping services. In the end, these accrued costs might leave the retail price of your goods on the high side.

In contrast, if you were to use freight forwarders, they already have a preset charge for your goods based on the weight of your product. Moreover, they come in and out of your country weekly if not every day. The frequency with which these freight companies, travel in and out of your country may differ from others, but the advantage this avails you is that you won't have to wait too long to get the delivery of your goods.

Furthermore, even if you want an express shipment of your goods you could make this happen at a relatively lower cost if you use freight forwarders. The amount you will be charged for their express service will be small compared with the ones you might pay if you had opted for DHL and the likes.

I will have you understand that timelines for delivery differ from one freight forwarder to another. Be clear that your shipping times align with your business goals.

Wait a minute; why the hurry? My advice is that you go for the normal shipping timeline offered by your freight forwarder. Except if there is an urgent need for the products, it may not be wise to accrue costs owing to express shipping. Consider the waiting time for your shipping the time to evaluate your sales plans and prepare for quick dispersal of your products. Use it as a time to prepare the market for your coming goods; create awareness while you wait, you could even pre-sell the products. It is possible! This will make your work easier when your shipment eventually arrives.

Order Tracking

Your order number is a unique number peculiar to your order on any e-commerce site you shopped. Its purpose is to make for easy identification of a specific order at any point in time.

In the course of waiting, buyers are often overcome by anxiety and would want to know the status of their goods. In order to ascertain this, you could simply log on to www.17track.net, copy your order number in the space provided and simply search for the order.

BUILDING RAPPORT WITH MANUFACTURERS/SUPPLIERS

What is the most important asset in your business? Do you consider it to be your product or service? Your building? Is it your machines and other capital infrastructure? Perhaps you think it is the money in the bank? Well, A big fat no to all of that. Your most important asset is the relationships you build along the way. Whether those be with customers, suppliers or others in your supply chain, these are more important than bricks and mortar.

If you want to put it in business terms, it is called social capital. Studies have shown how important building relationships can be when it comes to business. And I'm not just talking about the 'Hi. How can I help you?' type of relationship. Believe it or not, business relationships can be taken to a deeper level. I'm not talking about intimacy, but certainly to a level where trust and understanding, and even empathy comes into play. This will come in handy for you as you build your mini importation business.

Trust, of course, plays a massive role in building business relationships. Trust takes time to earn but can be thrown away in minutes. Suppliers and importers can quickly become opponents that were once allies. The late, famous salesman and public speaker, Zig Ziglar's quote says it all.

"If they like you, they will listen to you. If they trust you, they will do business with you."

Beyond ordering and payment for your orders, you should go the extra mile to build rapport and a long-term relationship with your supplier (even with your freight forwarders). Over time, you will begin to reap the invaluable benefits it avails, which include:

- Loyalty
- Early shipping timelines
- Access to value-added services
- Reduced costs
- Network opportunities
- Competitive advantage

Finally, on the dividends of building rapport with your supplier; most of the products you see on 1688.com and several other sites you might be using for your business always have a minimum order quantity (MOQ). This is the smallest units of a particular product you can cart at any one time. For certain times and purposes, the set MOQ may not be favourable to your business, in this case, all you need to do is fall back on your built relationship with the manufacturer to permit you to order even lower units than the MOQ.

We are almost there! Now you can successfully make the moneymaking orders. One more thing though; there is always the need to get the product into the hands of the needy consumers – your profits are embedded in selling not in the success of the arrival of your goods. The details of this are what I addressed in the next chapter.

Come on now; let us demystify selling.

CHAPTER 5

SELLING YOUR INVENTORY

For a lot of people, the challenge is that when the goods arrive, how will they sell the goods? Nonetheless, this is where they ought to be cashing in big. This is the time they are supposed to get bountifully rewarded for their 'labour' in bringing amazing products into their country to meet the needs and wants of a dire market.

If you want to be a make your desired profit from this business, you must be a great seller who differentiates from the others. You have to know what's working best and what isn't. Learn from other people's experiences and understand the techniques that help you sell products online or offline.

There is a need to demystify selling. You need to be sensitive to the various avenues around you that you can use to your advantage. At this stage of the business, the promotion of your merchandise is very important. There is a need for you to continually promote your products via word-of-mouth and other different social media platforms. Selling, of course, is actually very crucial in this business; if you don't promote your business, then you are sure to record low sales and your goods may begin to gather dust or even end up forgotten wherever you might have stored them.

IT BEGINS WITH PRICING

By providence, you have come across this invaluable information, and I have been able to reveal to you a wonderful site that can meet your product needs at a ridiculous amount. Therefore, your product pricing should be relatively affordable. That everyone is selling at a particular price does not mean you should retail at the same price. You can bring your price down to permit your entry into the market. The cheaper people see your product, the likelier they are to patronize you and the earlier you began to build a customer base.

Take the case of the e-commerce sites where you buy things normally, for example; you often come across a particular product priced differently on the same site; some are priced high while some are lowly priced. Online shoppers, nevertheless, are likely to go for the products with the lowest price. I want you to put this under advisement.

The reason for the price disparity of a particular product on the one e-commerce site is because there are different sellers retailing the product on that site. The price variation, therefore, results due to the difference in where each seller obtains his or her goods. The good news is that the opportunity to sell goods on existing e-commerce sites is available to anyone who is interested. One vital requirement is to have products to sell indeed. I will delve into the details of this soon, and I implore you to maximize this opportunity.

From the outset of my business, I have utilized the online marketplace for the disposal of my products and it has always fetched me a good profit. Before going into the detail of that, let me give you some tips about offline selling.

SELLING OFFLINE

Passion is one great force that unleashes creativity and creativity takes courage. For a blissful distribution of your products offline, you will be effective if only you are creative at it. Passion is magical; it will make you scale heights and surpass your business goals even before the set deadline. It is essential you unleash your passion while you are engaging in diverse kinds of promotion of your products to people offline. The reason for this is simple; nothing delivers beyond our level of sustained passion at it.

For a successful offline selling adventure, always bear in mind that there is a better way to do it and you must find it. Keep on improving on your innovation. You could find the following tips helpful:

- **Free Publicity**

Media sources are always looking for appealing stories – so why not yours? Contact your local newspapers, radio stations and television networks and provide interesting facts about you, your products and why you started your business. This will give drastic results if you have the products customized for you to bear perhaps your brand logo.

- **Affordable Newspaper Ads**

Most high schools and colleges have newspapers. If your product appeals to this demographic, these are excellent resources for low-cost advertising. In addition, you can approach most widely read papers and offer to buy any advertising space they can sell for a significantly reduced price.

- **Media Giveaways**

Radio and television stations are always looking for free products they can give away to their listeners and viewers. Offer to donate free products in exchange for advertisements and publicity about your company. This will work greatly whether or not you have your brand logo customized on the products or not. Your products get to be known, and the media producer/company may even become your loyal customers in no time.

- **Endorsements**

Give your products to prominent local, regional and national individuals for free. If they like it, they will use it, tell other people about it and maybe even endorse it formally. Now, this is a way to scale your business. Do not underestimate what this could do to your business.

Plus, this category of people is those that can afford your products even when you price it a little too high.

- **Networking**

Join clubs, business groups, and associations that attract prominent business leaders. Get to know people who may know potential customers for your business and ask if you can use their names in making calls.

- **Free Lunches**

Invite prospective customers to a free luncheon. This works well with business-to-business models. For a few hundred dollars, you can introduce potential buyers for your products and services. This takes the burden of retail off you. You get to sell your products in large quantities for an appreciable profit.

- **Vendor Trade Shows**

Go to vendor trade shows even if you cannot afford a booth. Sometimes you can split a booth with another company that sells compatible products. Many successful entrepreneurs attend trade shows with only prototypes and sell hundreds of products.

- **Trade Association Publications**

Nearly every industry association has a trade publication. These publications often feature new products and services and include interesting stories about entrepreneurs and new businesses in the industry. If the products you are dealing are not as common in your locality or city, you could use this to your advantage. The results you will get will amaze you.

- **Educational Workshops**

Hold a workshop that has educational value for potential customers. Your products and services can be included as a solution to the challenges they face. You must have a product that solves a particular problem in your city to make use of this avenue. For example, you stumbled upon a new electronic device on 1688.com which solve a big problem in your city, then, by all means, try out this tip.

- **Coupons, Flyers and Handouts**

With desktop publishing, you can create professional coupons, flyers and handouts for a very little cost. Distribute these from your place of business or from distribution points where potential customers congregate e.g. newspaper stands, restaurants, stadiums, etc.

- **Free Products**

Giving away your products for free is an excellent low-cost marketing strategy. This works well when you are selling low-ticket items people use regularly. Even when you are selling high-ticket products, you can always give away lower cost accessories and related items.

- **Direct Mail**

Direct mail can be an inexpensive strategy for targeting specific geographic markets. The cost per piece can be as little as 50 cents, and a 2 to 3 percent response rate can cover the entire cost of the campaign. You can also hire young people to deliver door hangers to potential customers in targeted markets.

- **Cross Promotions**

Cross promotions are popular in retailing, but can be used in any type of business. Find companies with related products or services, and then explore ways to promote each other's business. You can do this AT your respective business locations. Everybody wins!

Conclusively, be ready to sell yourself to your prospective customers; you have to reach out to them tirelessly via the word-of-mouth; the people in your network must know what you do and the products you are dealing. You have to press on this to a point that when they think of meeting a need, your name comes up because they know you have just the right product.

SELLING ONLINE

Anyone doing business in this century without having an online presence has barely started. Such a business will be drooling and will scarcely make significant progress. The internet has become part of our everyday life. Personally, I think it is very good to take one's business online because there are many benefits of doing business online over just having a real offline business. When you have an online business, billions of people can easily connect to you or your site. The influence of the internet continues to grow and every day more of us, and our businesses recognize the need for communicating and doing business online.

Nonetheless, you do not have to run your entire business over the internet to benefit from online business opportunities. Small businesses might only need an email address to communicate with their clients, customers and suppliers electronically. Other businesses might use their website to conduct their entire business online.

Concisely, the many benefits of online business include:

- Global access, 24 hours a day, 7 days a week

- Improved client service through greater flexibility

- Cost savings

- Faster delivery of products

- Increased professionalism

- Less paper waste

- The opportunity to manage your business from anywhere in the world.

Customers may prefer to visit your website to find out about your products and services, instead of visiting you in person. They will also expect to see your website address and your email on business cards and other promotional materials.

There are two ways of giving your business an online presence.

1. Setting up seller accounts with existing popular e-commerce sites in your country

2. Setting up your own e-commerce site.

HOW TO SET UP SELLER ACCOUNTS WITH EXISTING E-COMMERCE SITES

I quipped in the earlier part of this book that the internet is a deal breaker. It has charted a new course to how businesses are being run.

Basically, the following are what you may require before you are permitted to set up a seller account with some of the reputable e-commerce websites out there:

- A valid means of identification

- A valid email address

- Accurate bank information (that might have to be verified)

- A list of the items you intend to sell on the site and their respective categories

- Payment for selling plan (this is rarely charged by e-commerce sites)

Now you should understand that it is impossible for me to do an exhaustive listing and showing of how to sign up to start selling on the numerous existing e-commerce sites in different parts of the world. In the light of this I, will dwell on only a few specific cases.

SELLING TO AMAZON, SELLING ON AMAZON

With her global reputation, the size of Amazon's addressable audience is one of the amazing benefits that you are poised to enjoy by selling your products on their platform. Using Amazon's online marketplace as a channel for selling your products avails you the opportunity to price your cheaply procured quality goods at an almost same price as similar products are being sold. This will make for you, jaw-dropping profits.

Selling to Amazon:

This program allows sellers like you to sell to Amazon at wholesale price. You won't have to bother about the hassle of handling product pricing, shipping and other logistics for product sales. This takes a whole lot of stress off your shoulders and you get to receive your money without the needless passage of time.

Selling on Amazon:

More than half of total sales on Amazon come from third-party sellers. You will be required to list your products on the Amazon Marketplace, and sell items as a 3rd party seller.

However, selling on Amazon is generally more work than selling to Amazon; it nonetheless also comes with greater levels of control and the potential for higher profit margins. Sellers like you to the marketplace control shipping, prices and optionally order fulfillment.

Step 1:   Go to: services.amazon.com

Step 2:   Click on 'StartSelling'

Follow through with the instructions that come up on the next page and select a selling plan based on your budget.

For your profit maximization on Amazon, carefully set your selling price. Factor in all the charges and dues you had to pay to set up your store on Amazon so that you will not eventually run at a loss

SELLING ON eBay

Just like Amazon, one of the advantages that eBay avails you is access to showcase your products to the millions of active online shoppers registered on their site. With eBay, you get the opportunity to serve customers globally; when your stock is limited and the demand for your products is high, that is when you benefit from the auction listing on eBay. Get detailed information about eBay's auction listing to make the most of this opportunity.

Also, compared to Amazon, eBay actually charges lower fees for product listing.

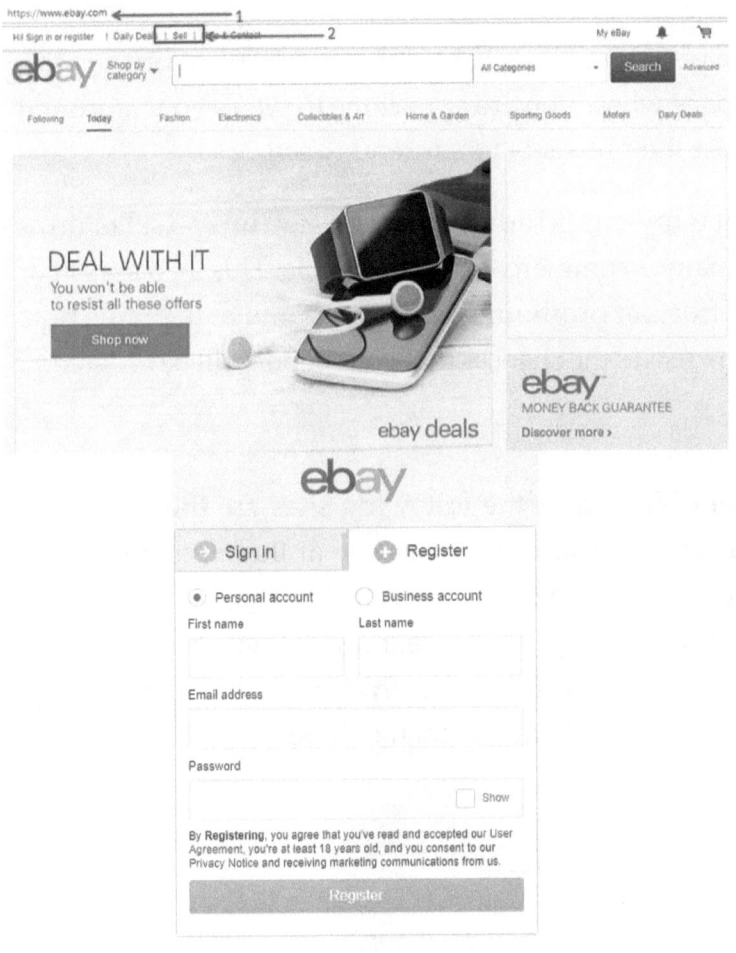

Step 1:   Log on to www.ebay.com

Step 2:   Click on sell

Step 3:   Fill the seller registration page as appropriate

Upon submitting the form, you will be redirected to a page where you are opportune to set up your store and list the products you intend to sell.

It is my candid advice that you sign up as a seller on as many e-commerce sites as possible. This increases your efforts at promoting your goods and at the same time increases the chances that your goods will be ordered.

For Nigerians, the following sites are the leading e-commerce sites in our nation at the moment. I have taken the time to walk you through the basic steps needed to sign up as a seller with them. Some of them have their peculiarities which I have endeavoured to share as I talk about each of them.

SELLING ON JUMIA

Step 1:   Go to www.sellercenter.jumia.com.ng

Step 2:   Click on 'Register to Sell'

Step 3:   Fill out the form on the page you are redirected to accurately

It takes about 24 – 48 hours for Jumia to verify your information and grant your request to set up a store with them. Thereafter, proceed to list your products and make sure you upload bright images of your products.

Jumia has a phenomenal seller support staff that always comes in handy anytime sellers (referred to as vendors) have an issue.

SELLING ON KONGA

Step 1:   Visit www.shq.konga.com

Step 2:   Click on Start Selling on Konga

Step 3:   You will be required to fill a form to include the niche of your products and your
                 store name.

Step 4:   Konga will conduct a test for you. You are expected to have above 80% on the
                 test before your store will be approved for operations.

Konga is actually unique in their operations and relations with the sellers on their site. They will attach each store owner to a support officer.

SELLING ON JIJI

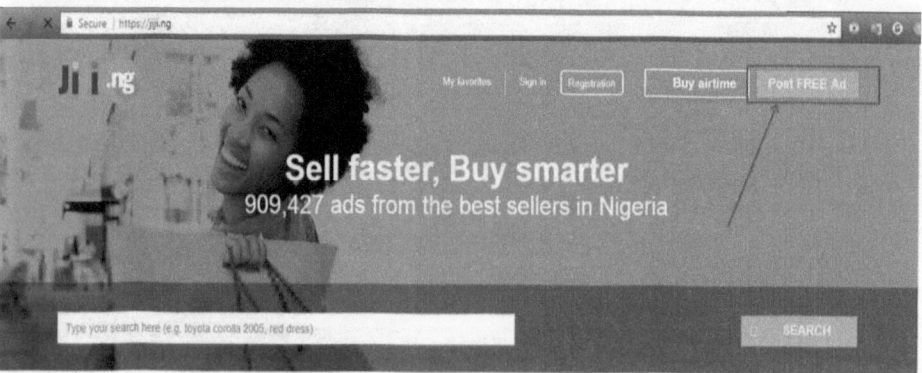

Click on the "Sign Up" button (you can choose either of 'post free ad' or click on sign up)

On Jiji, you can choose to register with Facebook directly or with your Google account. If you don't want to choose either of these options; then opt for the manual set up where you enter all the required information.

After the Sign Up, Jiji will suggest that you could decide to get more clients or post a free ad. It is easier to use a laptop. In all though, it is an easy process that a little kid can do. You then fill in the category and subcategory of the product you want to sell using the ad.

Next is the title and product description. The title should not be more than fifty words.

For those that are not in Nigeria but have roots in Nigeria, if you have a trusted relative or any other person you could trust, you can actually still set up a Jiji store.

If you are giving anyone the privilege to manage your Jiji account on your behalf, make sure you set up your bank account on the site using your own bank account information and not that of the person. Also, make sure you register on the site with two phone numbers, preferably, one belonging to each of you.

Jiji offers different selling plans. If you want to drive much traffic to your products, you can decide to subscribe for their premium plans. They have the $8.30 plan, $11.10 and the $13.90 plan from which you can choose. This actually helps you to drive much traffic to your Jiji account.

SELLING ON DEALDEY

Step 1: Go to www.merchant.dealdey.com

Step 2: Fill the required form and click 'Start Selling'

Step 3: List your products in their respective categories and await the activation of your store.

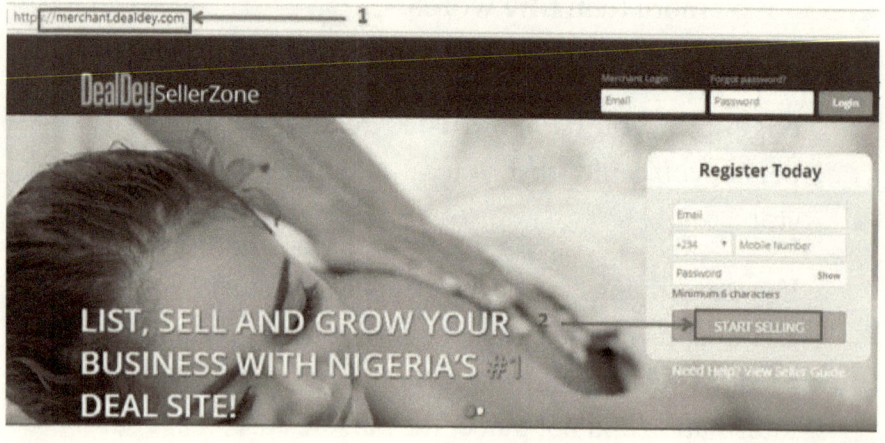

SELLING ON PAYPORTE

Payporte is also gradually becoming a household name when e-commerce is mentioned in Nigeria. Like the other e-commerce sites aforementioned, they also avail ordinary people with products to sell the opportunity to make their products available to their online audience.

The process involved is relatively easy compared to the others:

Simply visit www.payporte.com, on the home page, click on the 'Become a Seller' captain.

Fill in the required details; await the confirmation of your details and proceed to setting up your store.

Remember, the sites we have so far explored are not exhaustive. Endeavour to have your products on as many e-commerce websites as possible.

When it comes to selling online, especially products, you have to understand that clear, crisp pictures sell. A picture they say is worth more than 10,000 words. Pictures are the representation of your products on the e-commerce sites. Therefore, you have to make sure the pictures you are uploading on the e-commerce sites are bright, clear and of good quality.

The benign truth about using popular e-commerce sites as platforms to sell your merchandise is that sometimes the terms and conditions may not be as convenient and favourable to you. Moreover, some of these brands whose websites you are using to sell your products take time to remit your money to you long after they might have sold your products. Another issue of concern for sellers is the commission charged on products sold by these e-commerce sites. Some commissions are so high you have to alter the price of your good to the point that you stop having a competitive advantage.

This challenge will lead me to intimate you with another medium for selling your products you should carefully consider.

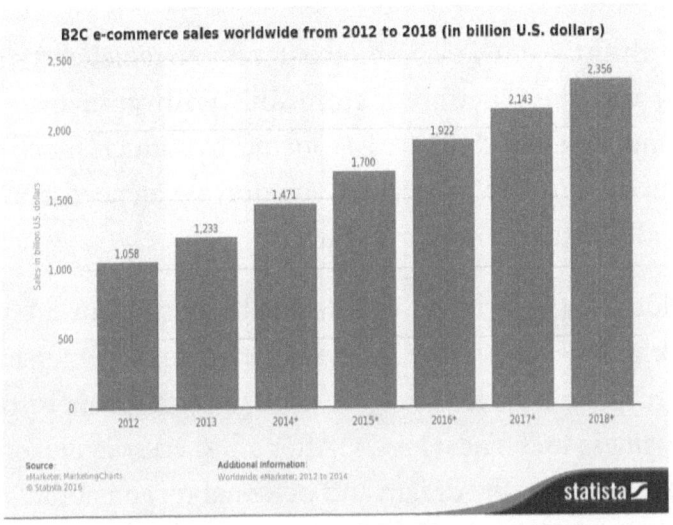

B2C e-commerce sales worldwide from 2012 to 2018 (in billion U.S. dollars)

HAVE YOUR OWN E-COMMERCE SITE

In my opinion, the biggest advantage is that doing business online expands your reach. You can be a tiny company and yet have customers all over the world. You not only help yourself; you also help those in need of your products, especially if what you are selling is not in abundance.

One of the most important decisions you can make as you venture into mini importation is to have an e-commerce website that you can call your own. That way, you become rid of the unnecessary limits and dues demanded of you by the e-commerce sites you may have been selling on before.

With all the other e-commerce stores you registered with all you have is only a store. But with your own e-commerce site, you can list a lot more products than you can squeeze in a store. Plus, you don't even need a brick and mortar store to get started.

More so, the moment you decide to set up your own e-commerce site you will develop a sense of ownership, which will serve as a powerful tool to propel your business to the next levels. After all, success is personal ownership of the dream and personal responsibility for its desired outcome.

Unlike what you may have presumed, setting up an e-commerce site has become relatively cheap and easy to do; thanks to continuous advancement in website programming. Now, anyone, anywhere, desirous of an e-commerce website can possess one for himself or herself. You can start your own online business without spending as much as you would to establish your offline business. This means that you can have success without dealing with all the financial hurdles and risks that are often associated with running a business the traditional offline route.

The following platforms are programs that have made setting up an e-commerce store really simple, easy and cost–effective.

To decide, to be at the level of your choice is to take responsibility for your business and to be in control of your business. There is a need for you to take some drastic steps after your e-commerce site has been set up. Utilizing the power of social media especially, you need to put the word out on your website. Run promotions, give discounts, give coupon codes and execute other creative ideas that have worked for others. Keep at this until your store becomes a well-known name for people in need of what your product niche offers.

USE THE VIRAL TOOL – SOCIAL MEDIA

During my mentoring several people on social media, I have come across people who would post all kinds of stories and pictures and videos of their social media accounts but not one thing about their merchandise and business. They are unknowingly losing cool cash. Instead, they crack unprofitable jokes, share posts made by other people to their own friends without making a profit off of it.

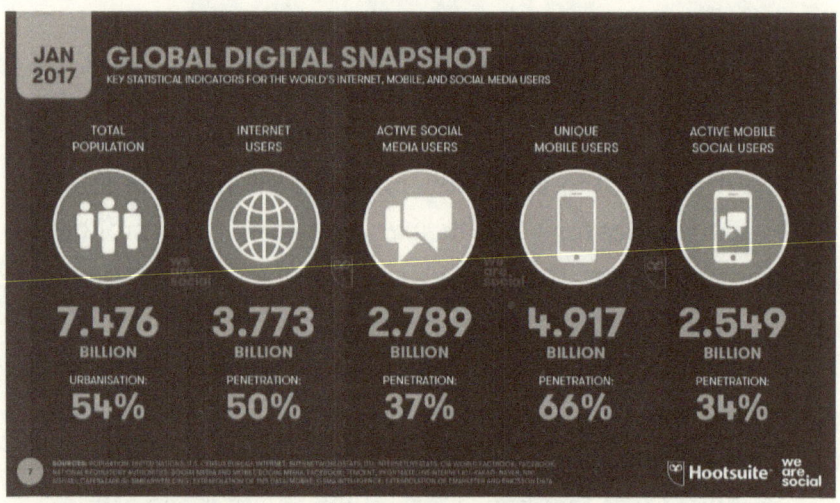

There are billions of people active at any particular time online and on the leading social media platforms.

To fully maximize the potential of this business, you will need to make judicious and wise use of social media. Use your social media accounts to your financial advantage; learn and implement social media marketing and online strategies. You will be amazed at how many people are willing to lay their hands on your products.

In fact, I make bold to say that if you want to always have a buy out of your products, then, social media can and will make this happen for you many times over. By all means, let this one big tool work its magic for your business.

As at 2016/2017, the data below holds true of the monthly users of the popular social media sites:

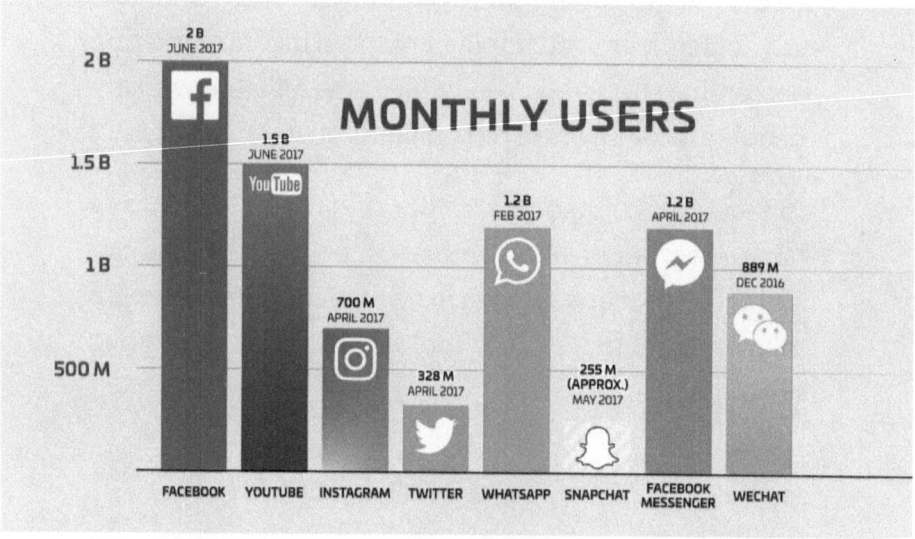

There is no need for you to delay the usage of this means of publicity for your business. It has been the beginning of a new dawn for many businesses. It does not matter what niche you are invested in; you are sure to find your customers on these social platforms. Go ahead; set up your business profiles on these platforms; let the massive sales begin.

When was the last time you got a mail in the mailbox in the front of your house? When was the last time you sent a mail via the post office? Lastly, when was the last time you could not wait to check your mailbox? I can only imagine the answer you gave to the questions above; it should go something like "I have not in a very long while."

Times are changing. Emails have taken the place of mails received in mailboxes now. Technology keeps changing the way things are being done. Billions of emails are being circulated daily. Just like many have, you could turn this to a profit-making medium for your business.

Email marketing is the act of sending a commercial message, typically to a group of people, using email. In its broadest sense, every email sent to a potential or current customer could be considered email marketing. It usually involves using email to send advertisements, request business, or solicit sales or donations, and is meant to build loyalty, trust, or brand awareness.

Marketing emails can be sent to a purchased lead list or an existing customer database. The term usually refers to sending email messages with the purpose of enhancing a seller's relationship with current or previous customers, encouraging customer loyalty and repeat business, acquiring new customers or convincing current customers to purchase something immediately, and sharing third-party ads.

Using appropriate applications like MailChimp, GetResponse, MailPrimo etc. you could start building an email list of people who had either patronized you or signed up for a newsletter on your site (or on any other platform as the case may be). It has been said repeatedly, the money is in the number of email addresses on your mailing list.

You keep sending product promotion emails; campaigns and notice of new-product arrival to people on your mailing list in the most professional manner as to avoid spamming. Since the phones of people on your list are always to their face, they will keep getting your emails which in turn will encourage them to patronize you. This is a brief of how email marketing works.

Get more workable information on this and ensure that you include it as one of the tools you will optimize for your business success.

CREATE A UNIQUE SELLING PROPOSITION

Why should people buy from you instead of patronizing others who are promoting the same product? Surely, your offer must have something special, something unique, something fabulous that will separate it from the rest. This distinguishing factor is your unique selling proposition.

A unique selling proposition (USP, also seen as a unique selling point) is a factor that differentiates a product from its competitors, such as the lowest cost, the highest quality or the first-ever product of its kind. A USP could be thought of as "what you have that competitors don't."

The USP, plain and simple, is the secret of the internet marketing millionaires. Anyone you see making amazing turnover from the sales of any product online has somehow formulated a unique selling proposition and compelled the public to buy from him/her.

The success of your online business will greatly depend upon the potency of the USP you are able to come up with. You should be able to personalize an offer to make your products better than the rest. You, of course, might not be selling a new product, but if you can add something that will make your offer better than the rest, you will naturally stand out amongst your competitors. People will notice you more and will buy more from you instead of the others.

For example, if you are selling a pack of Brazilian hair for say $85. If this also is the market price for the regular Brazilian hair out there, how then can you successfully make people patronize you instead of the others? The answer is simple: add something that will make your offer more valuable and there are a countless number of ways you can accomplish this.

An example might be that you decide to give away a nail polish and a lipstick for every Brazilian hair purchased from you. Bear in mind that if you are buying both the Brazilian hair and the freebies (nail polish and lipstick) from 1688.com, then you will be getting them at a ridiculously cheap price. Hence, it will not in any way amount to a loss on your part. Rather, it will earn you loyal customers in a jiffy.

Can you imagine what your sales will look like if you actually do this? The truth is that while others are yet cleaning dust off their packs of Brazilian hair, you will have a buy out in a matter of days and will be exhausted from the continuous orders you will be getting. Customers will literally beg you to buy from you. Never underestimate the power of free gifts as a USP; it works anywhere, any day like the talisman.

Now you are on a golden pedestal to kick-start your mini importation business. However, I have a final thought to share with you.

CHAPTER 6

CONGRATULATIONS!

If you have tried so hard to read this book to the end, neglecting the unending distractions around you; devoting your precious time to read the whole book and making it to the final chapter but you are yet to make a decision to start your own mini importation business, my question for you is:

What are you waiting for?

I encourage you to reflect on your goals and dreams; imagine the financial independence potential this business avails you and then genuinely ask yourself whether or not this business model can help you achieve your goals. Sincerely evaluate the whole idea again and know for sure if it will give you the financial independence you desire or not.

I have shared with you years' worth of my discoveries, tests, trials, trainings and the thousands of dollars I have spent to discover most of what I unveiled here. I have given these to you flat out. If you are not making concrete plans to start your mini importation business; if you are still dreaming and not taking action, then maybe this business is not for you in the first place.

Perhaps you are rest assured and lethargic because of your job. That will not work in the long run. Have you not been following the trend of things as the economy takes a nosedive? There is no such thing as job security anymore! With what I have unveiled to you, you are just one step away from being a successful entrepreneur. Embrace this opportunity and stop working at that job that you do not like; stand up for mini importation and say no to your beggarly minimum wage.

I have just handed you an opportunity, but remember, knowledge is only potential power. **Action is the real power**. I just gave a roadmap for a super successful mini importation business! If this doesn't excite you, I don't know what else possibly can. I don't know what else I could give you that would prompt you to start building your mini importation business.

If you don't take action, you might regret it. There is nothing worse than missing an opportunity that could have changed your life. To procrastinate action now is to delay your financial freedom. The market might become saturated soon. At that point, when you look back on this opportunity that you may not like yourself for taking a pass at this opportunity.

Do it! Stop watching TV! Let go of the banter you are always after on social media. Invest your time and resources in this business now. Did you not see? It does not cost so much to begin!

If this book ends up on your shelf collecting dust, then I would have failed. It is my utmost wish that you become one of the hundreds of my rags-to-riches success stories. I want to empower you! I want to change your life! I believe in the potential of this business to do so! In fact, I have a set goal to raise hundreds of mini importation millionaires by 2020.

I wrote this book only to extend the tremendous opportunity of mini importation to you. I firmly believe that every single person should be given this opportunity, but you need to take action!

As at the time of writing this chapter, one of my mentees in the business made her first sale of about $9,500 dollars from an investment of only $2360. In fact, the company that bought goods from her paid $3050 upfront. So it is okay to say that she invested nothing in the transaction. She was literally given the money to make the purchase of the goods in addition to her huge profit.

I have seen this happen many times in different fashions. This could be you too!

I really look forward to your success! I am positive I will share your success story on my platforms soonest.

Finally, I want to thank you from the bottom of my heart for reading this book and deciding to make the most of the information contained therein for your financial emancipation.

Last, but not least, **please take action**. I believe you are an entrepreneur. Every single individual reading this book is an entrepreneur. The only difference between successful people and unsuccessful people is opportunity, knowledge, and execution. I just gave you all three of those, right inside this book.

USE IT!

REFERENCES

INTRODUCTION

- *Mr Peter Kelvin is not the real name of my mentee.

CHAPTER 1

- http://www.entrepreneurshipinabox.com/80/market-research-what-is-it-benefits-process-and-information-sources/
- https://www.trainingindustry.com/articles/strategy-alignment-and-planning/advantages-of-ongoing-training-and-its-impact-on-employee-and-business-performance/
- https://www.cmtc.com/blog/the-benefits-of-adopting-a-continuous-improvement-approach
- https://www.mapi.net/blog/2015/09/china-solidifies-its-position-world's-largest-manufacturer
- https://en.wikipedia.org/wiki/International_trade
- http://www.nam.org/Newsroom/Top-20-Facts-About-Manufacturing/
  Source: Bureau of Economic Analysis
- http://www.globalization101.org/what-is-globalization/
- https://en.wikipedia.org/wiki/Import
- https://en.wikipedia.org/wiki/Trade_agreement

- https://en.wikipedia.org/wiki/List_of_countries_by_exports
- http://www.smallstarter.com/browse-ideas/how-to-start-a-small-scale-importation-business-in-africa/
- The 360° Leader – John C. Maxwell
- GOALS – Brian Tracy

CHAPTER 2

- www.apparelcandy.com
- www.599fashion.com
- www.lovelywholesale.com
- www.myntra.com
- www.amazon.com
- www.myus.com
- www.shoptomydoor.com
- www.dhgate.com
- www.cellularcountry.com
-

CHAPTER 3

- http://www.scmp.com/business/companies/article/2097691/alibaba-aims-become-fifth-largest-economy-2036
- http://www.jiesworld.com/international_corporations_in_china.htm
- https://en.wikipedia.org/wiki/Alibaba_Group

- www.alibaba.com
- www.aliexpress.com
- www.alipay.com
- www.1688.com
- www.taobao.com
- www.tmall.com
-

CHAPTER 4

- www.imqq.com
- www.17track.net

CHAPTER 5

- Fastest Ways to Make Money Online – Adewale Makanjuola
- https://www.business2community.com/sales-management/27-amazing-sales-facts-will-change-sell-01466377
- https://www.entrepreneur.com/article/284320
- http://www.thepartnermarketinggroup.com/demystifying-social-selling/
- https://www.quora.com/What-are-the-advantages-of-doing-business-online
- https://www.business.qld.gov.au/starting-business/internet-startups/online-basics/benefits
- http://interloperinc.com/what-are-the-advantages-of-doing-business-online/

- https://www.sensis.com.au/content/dam/sas/Article%20images/Infographicics/Sensis%20Social%20Media%20Report%20-%20sites%20used.jpg
- https://wearesocial-net.s3.amazonaws.com/uk/wp-content/uploads/sites/2/2017/01/Slide007.png
- https://en.wikipedia.org/wiki/Email_marketing

CHAPTER 6

- Starting From Zero – Fred Lam

About the Author

Adewale Makanjuola is a serial Net-entrepreneur, the President of Students' Intellectual and Moral Development Foundation (SIMDF) a non-governmental organization committed with the responsibility of moulding leaders of tomorrow.

He holds Bsc. Hon in Accounting from **Universite des Sciences Appliquees et Management Port-Novo (USAM), Benin Republic**.

Also an associate member of the Chartered Institute of Supply Chain Management, Ghana and Certified Institute of Warehousing and Material Management, Nigeria.

A philanthropist, and Nigeria No. 1 sought after Realtor who has helped top executives and busy professionals earn extra predictable income by investing disposable funds in real estate through the company LandPro Global Investments Limited.

A success coach, a prolific writer and bestselling author.
He's happily married to Evelyn, and both are blessed with four wonderful children, David, Sharon, Isaac and Goodness.

For Speaking Engagement, please write: princemjadewale@gmail.com **Tel:** +2348038484069

www.ingramcontent.com/pod-product-compliance
Lightning Source LLC
Chambersburg PA
CBHW030623220526
45463CB00004B/1397